THE CHILD'S

CHANGING CONSCIOUSNESS

As the Basis of Pedagogical Practice

[XVI]

FOUNDATIONS OF WALDORF EDUCATION

RUDOLF STEINER

The Child's
Changing Consciousness

As the Basis of Pedagogical Practice

& Anthroposophic Press.

The publisher wishes to acknowledge the inspiration

and support of Connie and Robert Dulaney

❖ ❖ ❖

In the collected edition of Rudolf Steiner's works in German, the volume containing these texts is *Die Pädagogische Praxis vom Gesichtspunkte geisteswissenschaftlicher Menschenerkenntnis* (vol. 306), published by Rudolf Steiner Verlag, Dornach, Switzerland, 1982. The lectures were translated by Roland Everett and edited by Rhona Everett; they have been revised for this edition.

Published by Anthroposophic Press,
RR 4 Box 94-A1 Hudson, N.Y. 12534

Library of Congress Cataloging-in-Publication Data to come

Steiner, Rudolf, 1861-1925
    [Padagogische Praxis vom Gesichtspunkte geisteswissenschaftlicher
Menschenerkenntnis. English]
    The child's changing consciousness as the basis of pedagogical practice /
Rudolf Steiner.
        p. cm. — (Foundations of Waldorf education : 16)
    "Translated from the German by Roland Everett and edited by
Rhona Everett"—T.p. verso.
    Includes bibliographical references and index.
    ISBN 0-88010-410-4
    1. Education—Philosophy. 2. Waldorf method of education.
3. Child development. 4. Anthroposophy. I. Title. II. Series.
    LB775.S7P3313   1996
    370'.1—dc20   96-33210

10 9 8 7 6 5 4 3

Printed in the United States of America

CONTENTS

What must happen for education to receive a new heart again? The intellectual age has reached a one-sided view of the human being. Its findings are based upon what becomes evident when the spiritual and some of the soul forces are left out of account. Many elements of an unreal soul constitution have crept into the present-day scientific viewpoint of the world. In order to reach the human being, living ideas are needed. In educational practice the whole life span of the human being needs to be considered.

Knowledge of the growing child—The first three faculties: walking, speaking, and thinking. In coming to terms with *statics and dynamics,* the weaving of destiny is hidden. From its environment the child absorbs the soul element of its surroundings. Through thinking it takes hold of outer nature.

Imitation as a natural law. Religious devotion toward the surrounding world. The widening of the horizon through the child's walking, speaking and first thinking. Approaching the artistic element through the medium of language. The child needs a pictorial, and not a logical approach. During the second life period acceptance of authority becomes a natural law. With the change of teeth memory begins to develop out of the child's ensouled life of habit. The interweaving of breathing and blood-circulation within the rhythmic system during the ninth and tenth years, and, through it, the child's taking hold of the musical forces. Puberty. The nature of the rhythmic system.

FOREWORD

Early in 1919 Rudolf Steiner was asked by the director of the Waldorf Astoria Tobacco Company in Stuttgart, Germany, to give lectures to the factory workers on the question of what new social impulses are necessary in the modern world. Responding to the lectures, the factory workers requested of Rudolf Steiner that he further help them in developing an education for their own children based on the knowledge of the human being and of society that he had opened up for them. By the end of April, that same spring, the decision had been made to establish a new school for the workers' children, the first Waldorf school.

Today, the Waldorf school movement, as it is still known (or the Rudolf Steiner school movement, as it is also called), is one of the largest, and perhaps the fastest growing, independent school movements in the world. In 1984 there were over 300 schools worldwide, throughout Europe, in the United States, Canada, South America, South Africa, Australia, and New Zealand. By 1995, the seventy-fifth anniversary of the Waldorf movement, there were over 600 schools in almost forty countries. Based on a comprehensive and integrated understanding of the human being, a detailed account of child development, and with a curriculum and teaching practice that seek the unity of intellectual, emotional, and ethical development at every point, Waldorf education deserves the attention of everyone concerned with education and the human future.

This book is a transcript of eight lectures plus an introduction to a eurythmy performance, taken originally in shorthand, given by Rudolf Steiner in April, 1923, at Dornach, Switzerland, to a group of Waldorf teachers and others from several European countries—he especially mentions the Czech representatives—who at this early stage had also become interested in Waldorf education. The reader today can readily sense the quality of active engagement that runs through these lectures as Rudolf Steiner explores the basic principles of Waldorf education, and at the same time, as required, confronts specific problems that arose in those early beginnings of the movement when the first school was not yet five years old. The reader is also carried immediately into a rich discussion of issues of central concern for education today. Perhaps the most helpful contribution this foreword can make to the reader is simply to underscore some of these issues.

Rudolf Steiner's holistic understanding of the human being underlies all of Waldorf education. To be sure, nearly every educational reform movement in the modern world claims to be concerned with "the education of the whole child," and in this way Waldorf education is no exception. In Waldorf education, however, this claim does not remain a generality. Rather, the many dimensions of the human being—physical, emotional, and intellectual, as well as the distinctive characteristics and myriad interrelationships of these dimensions—are presented with great care and precision. Further, their actual, concrete implications for the curriculum, the classroom, and the larger society are developed in detail and in a variety of ways.

In talking about the whole human being, Rudolf Steiner frequently employs the traditional terminology of body, soul, and spirit. Despite its venerable tradition, this terminology may, for many modern readers, strike a strange note at first, especially for most modern educators. And yet, those same readers will just as likely have no trouble at all with the original Greek term for "soul," *psyche*, which has acquired a firm and familiar place in the modern vocabulary just as its more recent equivalent, *soul*, has become somewhat strange and unfamiliar. And "psychosomatic" is the *au courant* expression for a sophisticated awareness of the mind-body relationship and its interaction—a term that is, however, seldom spelled out, and that often covers more than it reveals. The attentive reader will find that Rudolf Steiner makes use of traditional terminology in a precise, truly nontraditional way to explore and delineate essential dimensions and functions of the human being, which the fashionable Greek of *psyche* and *psychosomatic* tend to generalize and blur, and which much modern educational literature ignores altogether. At the very least the reader is well-advised to work with the traditional terminology and test whether or not it is indeed being used with precision and with real efficacy.

Rudolf Steiner does not, however, limit himself by any means to traditional terminology. Many readers will immediately find themselves on familiar ground with Steiner's detailed account of child development. And they may recognize that many aspects of Steiner's description have been subsequently confirmed, and in certain areas filled out, by educational and developmental psychologists working independently of him (Gesell and Piaget come to mind). Readers may also notice some important differences that, together with obvious areas of overlap, invite more dialogue between Waldorf educators and non-Waldorf educators than has yet occurred. Likewise, the crucial importance that Steiner attributed to the early, preschool years—particularly as it relates to an individual's entire life—has since become a commonplace of almost all developmental psychology. No one, however, has explored the educational implications of these early years with the fullness and care for actual curriculum and classroom practice that marks Steiner's work. One example in these lectures is the care he gives to describing the educational and developmental importance of the child's learning to stand and walk, to speak, and to think—all on its own—and the unfolding implications that he indicates these early achievements have for the whole of an individual's life.

Central to Steiner's account of child development is that the child comes to know the world in ways that are specific to the physical age and development of the child, and which serve as an essential foundation for other ways of knowing that follow. The primary way, Steiner points out, by which the very young, pre-school age child comes to know the world and others is through physical, sensory activity. This is an immediate, participative way of knowing by which the child through physical activity, and above all, through imitation, emulation, and play first comes to know and to make the world its own.

There are many interesting potential points of contact between Steiner's description of the child's participative, imitative knowing, and the independent investigations accomplished since his death by others unacquainted with either Steiner's more general work or Waldorf education; these points of contact also offer the promise of a fruitful exchange between Waldorf education and others. For example, the importance, stressed by Steiner, of play, imitation, and activity as being the foundation for all subsequent knowing, even that of formal analytic cognition, which comes into its own with adolescence, has been explored in great detail by many developmental psychologists. Kurt Fischer, for instance, writes, "All cognition starts with action ... the higher-level cognition of childhood and adulthood derive directly from these sensorimotor actions...." And Piaget, early in his work wrote, "At this most imitative stage, the child mimics with his whole being, identifying himself with his model." Many years before, in the lectures reprinted here, and with the actual implications for education much more at the center of his concern, Rudolf Steiner, in a stunning expression, said that "the young child, in a certain sense, really is just one great sense organ," imitating and absorbing its whole environment.

The kind of deep knowing Steiner describes here seems akin to the kind of knowing that the philosopher of science Michael Polanyi described later in terms of "tacit knowing": a knowing-by-doing, a knowing that exists primarily in what psychologist Lawrence Kubie, and others, have called the "pre-conscious."

Moreover, Steiner's conception expressed in these lectures of the young child as "a sense organ" in which will forces are at work connects directly with all those investigators in the field of phenomenology for whom intentionality, or will, is central to all experience, including perception. As Steiner also emphasizes, this early participative knowing of the child encompasses the moral and the religious, because it involves participation with the environment, with other people, and with one's own experience in being. It is a kind of knowing that involves the being of the knower, and it is the essential foundation for what Philip Phenix has called, "learning to live well as persons." It is a genuine knowing, which, as both Polanyi and Steiner stress, is always presupposed by more abstract, intellectual knowing. Indeed, Rudolf Steiner's description of the child's first experience of mathematics provides a vivid illustration of this crucially important point. Steiner indicates how the young child has first a lived, but pre-conscious experience of mathematics in its own early physical movements, an experience Steiner nicely describes as "bodily geometry," a lived experience which then becomes the basis for the eventual development of abstract, mathematical conceptual thinking later on. It becomes clear how the full development of this pre-conscious, tacit knowing, grounded in lived experience is essential to the emergence of truly powerful and insightful abstract conceptuality in later years.

More than any others who have dealt with it, Rudolf Steiner developed in considerable detail the implications of the young child's participative, tacit knowing (to use Polanyi's term for education). Positively, it means that the educator's primary task for the pre-school child is to provide an environment and people worthy of imitation by, and interaction with, the child. Negatively, it means that every attempt to teach young children analytical, conceptual thinking—the wide-spread efforts to teach reading, calculating, and computer skills at an ever earlier age—is premature, and a destructive intrusion that threatens the full development of the tacit knowing so necessary for truly powerful, creative, and self-confident thinking in later life. Although the dominant tendency in modern education is to continue to "hot house" young children to acquire adult reading and calculating skills, some important educators, like David Elkind, are beginning to point out, as Waldorf schools have always done, how destructive this is to the child's eventual educational growth and even physical health.

In the primary school years, Rudolf Steiner points out, the child enters a new stage when the feeling life becomes dominant. The child lives in feelings, and these now become the child's primary way of knowing the world—through the feeling, pictorial, rich image-making capacities that the rhythmic, feeling life makes possible. One can say, perhaps, that while the intelligence of the pre-school child first awakens in the physical life of the child, the intelligence of the child in primary school now awakens mainly in the life of feelings. Steiner explicitly identified these years when the imagination emerges as central between the child's change of teeth and puberty. A few educators have apparently begun to recognize that the change of teeth may, indeed, be an important signal that the child is entering upon a new level of development. It is, Steiner said, a signal that the child's forces, previously involved in physical growth, now become available in a new way for imaginative thinking, and, therefore, need to be nourished and cultivated imaginatively.

It is here that we see the importance of the image in all thinking. Whenever we want to explain, understand, or integrate our experience, we must have recourse to our images. Our images give us our world, and the kind and quality of our world depends on the kind and quality of the images through which we approach and understand it. During the school years when the child lives and knows the world through an imaginative, feeling life, a powerful image-making capacity is either developed or not. It is this vital picture-making capacity that gives life and insight to logical and conceptual thinking. The primary task of education in the primary school years is, therefore, to educate and nourish the imaging powers of the child, and to lead him or her into the development of strong, flexible, and insightful conceptual capacities, which only developed imagination makes possible.

Here the moral dimension in knowing and education appears in yet another way. We are responsible for the kind of images we bring to bear on the world, and the ways we do it. And we are responsible for the care we take in helping children to develop their own strong image-making capacities. Much in modern American education, with its nearly exclusive emphasis on utilitarian, problem-solving skills, neglects entirely the development of the child's imagination. At the same time— through television, movies, literalistic picture books, and detailed toys, all of which leave nothing to the child's own imaginative powers—the children are made increasingly vulnerable to having their minds and feelings filled with ready-made, supplied images—other people's images, often of the most banal, even violent and obsessive kind.

Steiner stresses, therefore, the importance of an education during the primary school years that is thoroughly artistic in nature. In these lectures he explicitly criticizes any one-sided emphasis on emotional development that ignores the importance of intellectual development. He also criticizes as nonsense notions that all learning should be play. (In this he transcends the current split between the partisans of so-called cognitive education and affective education.) Rather than emphasizing artistic as opposed to intellectual subjects, his chief concern is to bring together intellect, emotion, and the tacit knowing of will activity in an integral unity. Every subject, especially including mathematics and science, therefore, is to be presented in an imaginative, artistic way that speaks to and nourishes the child's own imagination. In the education sought in Waldorf schools, sound, tone, stories, poetry, music, movement, handwork, painting and colors, and direct acquaintance with living nature and other people permeate the pedagogy and the curriculum of these primary school years.

It is just such an artistic education in this fullest sense that leads to strong conceptual powers in the adolescent and adult years. Other people, such as the philosophers Alfred North Whitehead and John Macmurray, have recognized the centrality of the imaging, feeling life of the primary school child, and have urged that an artistic sensitivity and approach characterize all teaching during these years. Even John Dewey, in one of his more recent books, *Art as Experience*, and in some later essays, speaks of art as the primary model for all knowing, and of the importance of conceiving of "education as an art." In these writings Dewey saw how essential an artistic education is to all

thinking. Dewey wrote: "... the production of a work of genuine art probably demands more intelligence than does most of
the so-called thinking that goes on among those who pride
themselves on being intellectuals." But Dewey never developed
the educational implications of his own recognition of the centrality of the artistic-imaginative experience, and American
education—although it has been enamored with Dewey's
other, narrower stress on problem-solving skills—has totally
ignored his later emphasis on artistic imagination and education as an art. Only now are there signs, as in the work of Elliot
Eisner, that some educators are beginning to recognize how
essential an artistic, imaginative approach in education is.
Here, once again, Waldorf education, with its seventy-five years
of experience, can make an essential contribution to the current educational dialogue. At a time when increasing numbers
of Americans are concerned that our schools do everything
necessary to develop genuinely self-confident and creative
thinking, the importance of the attention given in Waldorf
education to the deepest sources of imagination, creativity, and
self-confidence becomes more and more apparent.

Perhaps two other elements in these lectures, which speak
directly to current American educational concerns, should be
briefly discussed. One has to do with the demand of many parents and public figures today that new attention be given in
American schools to religious and moral education, and what is
often called "teaching values." In these lectures Rudolf Steiner
stresses the importance of thinking about religious and moral
education in a way very different from what is customary. At
certain points in these lectures the reader will note that Rudolf
Steiner and the first Waldorf schools had to grapple with difficult, specific problems posed by the current legal requirements
in Germany regarding religious instruction. Even in the discussion of these specific issues, it is clear that Rudolf Steiner rejects

any form of indoctrination or empty teaching of abstract religious concepts. Rather, he emphasizes the importance of the teacher. The child brings into life in its earliest years a natural gratitude for being—what Steiner suggestively terms a kind of natural "bodily religion." And the religious-ethical task of the teacher is to respond in kind—to make available to the child an environment of things, people, and attitudes worthy of the child's grateful imitation; "the task of the teachers is through their actions and general behavior" to create a trustworthy reality for the children to live in.

As the imaginative life flowers in the primary school child, the fundamental ethical-religious education is again to be sought in providing the children with an experience of beauty, fairness, a reverence for life, and a life-giving attitude and conduct on the part of the teacher. The truly ethical and religious dimensions of education have nothing to do with indoctrination, the teaching of empty concepts, "thou-shalt" attitudes, but with the actual experience of gratitude, love, wonder, a devoted interest in one's life tasks and conduct, and a recognition of the worth of the developing individual. Instead of concerning ourselves so much with teaching the children moral concepts, writes Steiner, "we should strive towards a knowledge of how we, as teachers and educators, should conduct ourselves."

And this points to another current concern within American education; namely, the need to recognize the essential importance of the person and being of the teacher (and the parent) in education. Many recent calls for reform in American education have pointed to the low standing of the teacher in our culture, and the necessity of rectifying this. In these lectures, as elsewhere, Rudolf Steiner has much of crucial importance to say. In this regard, his discussion of the complex, and necessary relationships between the child's experience of genuine authority (not authoritarianism) and the development of freedom and capacity for self-determination in later life is especially pertinent to current educational concerns.

It should, perhaps, also be noted in concluding that in these lectures Rudolf Steiner was speaking to people who had at least an acquaintance with the view of the human being, on which his lectures were based. Occasionally, therefore, the word *anthroposophy* appears without explanation, and the reader who is meeting Rudolf Steiner and Waldorf education for the first time may have difficulty understanding what is meant. *Anthroposophy* was the term Rudolf Steiner used to characterize the approach to understanding the whole human being as body, soul, and spirit; while at first foreign to the modern eye, a moment's reflection will show that the term is no more difficult than the more familiar word, *anthropology*, except that, instead of the Greek word, *logos*—or "wisdom"—*sophie* is joined with the Greek word for "human being"—or *anthropos*. Elsewhere, Steiner expressed his hope that anthroposophy would not be understood in a wooden and literal translation, but that it should be taken to mean "a recognition of our essential humanity." The ground of Waldorf education is precisely this recognition of the essential human being. Central to Waldorf education is the conviction that each pupil, each person, is an individual, evolving self of infinite worth—a human spirit, for the essence of spirit, Steiner insisted, is to be found in the mystery of the individual self. As the English Waldorf educator John Davy once observed, this is not a fashionable view in a skeptical age, but it is one that carries a natural affinity with all who care about the education and evolving humanity of our children.

This foreword has attempted only to touch on some of the riches to be found in these lectures. Yet, this lecture cycle itself is far from an exhaustive account of Waldorf education. For those who want to explore further, the following lecture cycles by Rudolf Steiner are especially recommended as introductions to Waldorf education: *The Education of the Child and Early Lectures on Education*; *The Spirit of the Waldorf School*; and *The Kingdom of Childhood*. Steiner delivered other lecture series on education that require a deeper familiarity with Waldorf education and anthroposophy.[1] Introductions to Waldorf education by others are also especially recommended: Mary Caroline Richards, "The Public School and the Education of the Whole Person" contained in *Opening Our Moral Eye*; A. C. Harwood, *The Recovery of Man in Childhood: A Study in the Educational Work of Rudolf Steiner*; Majorie Spock, *Teaching as a Lively Art*; and Frans Carlgren, *Education Towards Freedom*. Useful introductory articles will also be found in "An Introduction to Waldorf Education," *Teachers College Record*, vol. 81 (Spring 1980): 322–370.

DOUGLAS SLOAN
Teachers College,
Columbia University

---

1. See pp. 210-211 for a more comprehensive list of titles.

THE CHILD'S

CHANGING CONSCIOUSNESS

As the Basis of Pedagogical Practice

Lecture One

Ladies and Gentlemen,

Dear Friends,

At the opening of this conference, I want to extend my warmest greetings to you all. Had you come some four or five months earlier, I would have welcomed you in the building we called the Goetheanum, which stood over there. The artistic forms of its architecture and its interior design would have been a constant reminder of what was intended to go out into the world from this Goetheanum. However, the misfortune that befell us on New Year's night and inflicted such grievous pain on all who loved this building, has robbed us of the Goetheanum. And so, for the time being, we shall have to nurture the spirit—without its proper earthly home—that would have reigned within this material, artistic sheath.

It gives me great joy to welcome those of you who have come from Switzerland, and who have displayed, through your coming, real evidence of your interest in our educational goals, even though they have been received recently in Switzerland with enmity. With equal joy and gratification I want to welcome the many friends of Waldorf Education—or those wishing to become its friends—who have come from Czechoslovakia. Your presence confirms to me that education involves one of the most crucial questions of our time, and that it will receive the impetus it needs and deserves only if it is seen in this light by the various members of the teaching profession.

Furthermore, I welcome those of you who have come from other countries, and who show, through your presence, that what is being worked toward here in Dornach is not just a matter of cosmopolitan interest, but is also a matter of concern for all of humanity.

And finally I want to greet our friends, the teachers of the Waldorf School. Their primary goal in coming here is to contribute to this conference from their own personal experience. They are deeply connected with our cause, and expressed the wish to support this conference. This is greatly appreciated.

Today, as an introduction, I want to prepare the ground for what will concern us during the next few days. Education is very much in the news today, and many people connected with educating the young are discussing the need for reform. Many different views are expressed—often with considerable enthusiasm—about how education should go through a change, a renewal. And yet, when hearing the various ideas on the subject, one cannot help feeling a certain trepidation, because it is difficult to see how such different views could ever lead to any kind of unity and common purpose, especially since each viewpoint claims to be the only valid one.

But there is another reason for concern. New ideas for education do not cause undue concern in themselves, for the necessities of life usually blunt the sharp edges, causing their own compensations. When one hears nearly everyone call for a renewal in education, yet another problem comes to mind—that is, where does this praiseworthy enthusiasm for better education spring from?

Isn't it prompted by people's memories of unhappy childhood days, of their own deep-seated memories of an unsatisfactory education? But as long as the call for educational reform comes only from these or similar feelings, it merely serves to emphasize personal discontent with one's own schooling. Even if certain educational reformers would not admit this to themselves or to others, by the very nuance of their words they imply dissatisfaction with their own education. And how many people today share this dissatisfaction! It is little wonder if the call for a change in education grows stronger every day.

This educational dilemma, however, raises two questions, neither of which is comforting. First, if one's education was bad, and if as a child one was exposed to its many harmful effects, how can one know what constitutes proper educational reform? Where can better ways of educating the young be found? The second question arises from listening to what certain people say about their own education. And here I want to give you a practical example because, rather than presenting theories during this conference, I want to approach our theme in practical terms.

A few days ago a book appeared on the market that, in itself, did not draw my particular interest. Nevertheless it is interesting because in the first few chapters the author, an outstanding person who has become world-famous, speaks very much about his early school days. I am referring to the memoirs of Rabindranath Tagore,[1] which have just been published. Although I do not have the same interest in this person that many Europeans do, in regard to educational matters his memoirs do contain some noteworthy and pertinent details.

I am sure that you would agree that the most beautiful memories of one's early school days—however wonderful these may have been—will hardly consist of fragmentary details of what happened in certain lessons. Indeed, it would be sad if this

---

1. Rabindranath Tagore (1861–1941) Indian Bengali poet and novelist; won Nobel prize for literature in 1913; knighted by England, but resigned knighthood (1919) in protest against English repression in Punjab.

were so, because what affects children during lessons should become transformed into life habits and skills. In later life we should not be plagued by the details of what we once learned at school, for these must flow together into the great stream of life. Couldn't we say that our most beautiful recollections of school are concerned with the different teachers we had? It is a blessing if, in later years, one can look back with deep, inner satisfaction at having been taught by one or another admired teacher. Such an education is of value for the whole of one's life. It is important that teachers call forth such feelings in their pupils; this also belongs to the art of education.

If we look at some of the passages in Tagore's memoirs from this perspective, we find that he does not talk of his teachers with much reverence and admiration. To quote an example, he says, "One of our teachers in the elementary school also gave us private lessons at home. His body was emaciated, his face desiccated, and his voice sharp. He looked like a veritable cane." One might easily imagine—especially here in our Western civilization, often criticized strongly in the East—that the wrongs of education would hardly be so vehemently emphasized by an Asian. But here you have an example of how an Eastern personality, now world-famous, looks back at his school days in India. And so I shall use a word that Tagore also mentions in his book—that is, "miserable school." The meaning of this expression is not confined to European countries, but seems to express a worldwide cultural problem. Later on we shall have to say much more about what teachers must do to kindle genuine interest for what they bring to their pupils.

But now I shall give you another example from Tagore's memoirs of how his English teacher approached this task. Tagore writes, "When I think back on his lessons, I cannot really say that Aghor Babu was a hard taskmaster. He did not rule us with the cane." To us, such a remark would point to times long past, long superseded. The fact that Tagore speaks so much in his book about the cane indicates something we would consider culturally primitive. I believe that such a comment is justified when reading Tagore's description, not just about one of his teachers "looking like a veritable cane," but also when he points out that another teacher actually did *not* use the cane. Speaking of this other teacher, Tagore continues, "Even when reprimanding us he did not shout at us. But, whatever his positive sides may have been, his lessons were given in the evening, and his subject was English. I am sure that even an angel would have appeared to a Bengali boy like a true messenger of *Mamas* (The God of Death), had he come to him in the evening after the 'miserable school' of the day, kindling a comfortless, dim lamp, in order to teach English."

Well, here you have an example of how a famous Indian speaks about his education. But Tagore also writes about how each child brings certain needs to education. He points out in a very practical way how such needs should be met, and how this did not happen in his case. I will leave it to you to interpret this situation in Western terms. To me it seems very good to look at such matters from a global perspective, matters that—if quoted in a European context—could very well arouse strong criticism. Tagore continues:

From time to time Aghor Babu tried to introduce a refreshing scientific breeze into the dry routine of the class room. One day he pulled from his pocket a little parcel wrapped in paper, saying, "Today I want to show you one of the Creator's wonderful works of art." Unwrapping the paper, he showed a human larynx, which he used to explain to us the wonders of its mechanism.

I still remember the shock this gave me, for I had always thought that speech came from the entire human being. I did not have the slightest inkling that the activity of speaking could thus be isolated from the whole human organism. However perfect the mechanism of each single part might be, surely it would always amount to less than the complete human being. Not that I consciously realized this, but at the bottom of my feelings it was distasteful. The fact that the teacher had lost sight of such a truth must have been the reason why his pupil could not share in his enthusiasm for this kind of demonstration.

Well, this was the first shock when the nature of the human being was introduced to the boy. But another one, worse still, was to follow. Tagore continues:

On another occasion he took us into the dissecting room of the local medical school. [There can be no doubt that Aghor Babu wanted to give his boys a special treat.] The corpse of an old woman was lying on a table. This in itself did not particularly disturb me. But an amputated leg, which was lying on the floor, completely threw me off my balance. The sight of a human being in such a state of fragmentation seemed so dreadful, so utterly lacking in sense to me, that I could not shake off the impression of this dark and expressionless leg for many days to come.

This example illustrates the reaction of a young person introduced to anatomy. Fundamentally speaking, this procedure is adopted in education only because it is in line with the orthodox scientific approach. And since the teacher has indeed gone through scientific training, it is naturally assumed to be a wonderful idea to demonstrate the mechanics of human speech with a model of the larynx, or to explain physiological anatomy with the aid of an amputated leg, for contemporary scientific thinking does not consider it necessary to look at the human being as a whole.

However, these are not yet the primary reasons for selecting certain passages from Tagore's memoirs—of which we will say more later on, not because of their connection with Tagore, but because they belong to the theme of our conference. First, I want to make another point.

Anyone judging Tagore's literary merits will correctly recognize in him an outstanding individual. In the autobiography of this distinguished author we read about his dreadful education. Doesn't this encourage a strange thought—that his poor education did not seem to harm his further development? Couldn't one conclude that a thoroughly bad education doesn't necessarily inflict permanent or serious harm? For did Tagore not demonstrate that despite this, he was able to grow into a good, even a famous person? (Examples like this could be multiplied by the hundreds, though they may be less spectacular.)

Considering the myriad impulses for educational reform, one could easily be pulled in two directions. On the one hand, how can anyone possibly be in a position to improve education if one has had the misfortune of suffering from a bad one? On the other hand, if "miserable school" has not prevented someone from becoming, not just a good, but even a great and famous person, then a bad education cannot do permanent harm. Is there any point in lavishing so much care on attempts to improve education? From a superficial perspective, one might conclude that it would be better to occupy oneself with matters that are more useful than educational reform.

If anthroposophy, which has been much maligned, were merely to offer even more ideas for educational reform, as is generally done, I would not even consider it worthwhile to attempt these in practice. But in reality, anthroposophy is something very different from what most people imagine it to be, for it springs from the deepest needs of our present culture. Anthroposophy does not proceed, as so many of its enemies do, by shamefully denigrating everything that does not agree with its own principles. Anthroposophy is more than prepared to recognize and acknowledge what is good, wherever it is found. More of this later, for, as I have said already, today's content is intended only as an introduction.

Anthroposophy points to the importance of the scientific achievements of the last three to four centuries and, above all, to those of the nineteenth century, all of which it fully recognizes. At the same time, however, anthroposophy also has the task of observing how these great scientific successes affect the human soul. It would be foolish to think that the ideas of a relatively few scientifically trained experts have little consequence for society as a whole; for even people who know little or nothing about science are influenced by contemporary science in their soul mood and in their life's orientation. Even people of a strictly orthodox religious faith, born of tradition and habit, nevertheless owe their world orientation to the results of orthodox science. The attitude of modern people is colored increasingly by the scientific view with all its tremendous achievements, which cannot be praised highly enough.

Yet the constitution of the human soul has been strangely affected by modern science. Having revealed more and more of outer nature, science has, at the same time, alienated human beings from themselves. What happens when the human being is observed from a scientific perspective? Our attention is drawn first to what has already been discovered very thoroughly in the inert, lifeless world. Then the human being is analyzed according to physiological and chemical components and what was established in the laboratories is then applied to the living human being.

Or else our attention is directed to other realms of nature, to the plant and animal kingdoms. Here scientists are fully aware that they have not been able to establish laws as convincing as those applied to inorganic nature. Nevertheless—at least in the animal realm—what has been discovered is then also related to the human being. This is the reason why "the man in the street" sees the human being as the final evolutionary stage of animals. The evolutionary ladder of the animal species ends with the emergence of the human being. The animals are understood up to a certain point. Their bony structures or muscular configurations are then simply transferred to the human being who, as a result, is considered to represent the most developed animal.

As yet, no true picture of the human being has arisen from these methods, and this will become poignantly clear to us when we focus on education. One could say that whereas in earlier times human beings occupied a central position within the existing world order, they have been displaced, crushed by the weight of geological data, and eliminated from their own sphere by the theory of animal evolution. Merely to trace back one of the ossicles of the human middle ear to the square-bone *(Quadratbein)* of a lower animal is praised as real progress. This is only one small example, but the way human physical nature reflects the soul and spiritual nature seems to have been entirely disregarded by modern research.

This kind of thing easily escapes notice, because the orthodox approach is simply taken for granted. It is a by-product of our modern culture, and properly so. Indeed, it would have been a sad situation if this change had not occurred, for, with the soul attitude that prevailed before the age of science, humanity could not have progressed properly. Yet today a new insight into human nature is called for, insight based on a scientific mode of thinking, and one that will also shed light on the nature of the entire universe.

I have often tried to show how the general scientific viewpoint—which in itself, can be highly praised—nevertheless can lead to great illusions, simply because of its innate claims of infallibility. If one can prove science wrong on any specific point, the whole thing is relatively simple. But a far more difficult situation arises when, within its own bounds, a scientific claim is correct.

Let me indicate what I mean. What led to a theory such as that of Kant-Laplace?[2] Using this theory—which has been modified recently, and is known to practically every educated person—scientists attempt to explain the origin of our Earth and planetary system. In their calculations, some of these scientists went back over long periods of time. When one scientist spoke of some twenty million years, soon enough he was considered naïve by others who spoke in terms of two hundred million years. Then other scientists began to calculate the length of time of certain processes taking place on Earth today. This is a perfectly correct thing to do, because from a strictly material point of view there is nothing else one can do. Sedimentation or metamorphosis of rocks was observed and, from the data gained, a picture was built up that explained certain changes, and the length of time involved was then calculated. For example, if the waters of Niagara Falls have been falling on the rocks below for such and such a period of time, one can calculate the degree of erosion of these rocks. If one now transfers this calculation to another spot somewhere else where considerably more erosion has been found, one can calculate the time this must have required through simple multiplication. Using this method, one might arrive at, let's say, twenty million years, which is quite correct as far as the calculation is concerned.

---

2. Pierre Simon Marquis de Laplace (1749–1827) French astronomer and mathematician. Immanuel Kant (1724–1895) German philosopher.

Similarly, one may start with the present time and, according to another well-known theory, calculate the time it will take for the Earth to become subject to heat death, and so on.

Yet, such a procedure might equally well be applied to a very different situation. Observe, for example, how the human heart changes from year to year. Noting the differences, one could investigate—following the same method applied in the case of Niagara Falls—how this heart must have looked some three hundred years ago, and what it would look like some three hundred years from now. Technically speaking, this method would be analogous to that of determining the times of geological changes and in this sense it would be correct. Observing the heart of a person aged about thirty-five, one would be basing one's calculations on an organ that has been functioning for a considerable length of time. However, one obvious detail has been overlooked—that this particular heart did not exist three hundred years ago, nor will it be there three hundred years from now. Though mathematically speaking the calculation is correct, it has no relationship to reality.

In our current intellectual age we are too preoccupied with whether or not something is correct, whether or not it is logically correct; but we have lost the habit of asking whether it conforms to actual real-life situations. We will confront this problem again and again this week. But it can happen sometimes that, when we follow apparently correct theories, even fundamental issues are simply overlooked. For example, you may have witnessed—I am not implying that as teachers you have actually carried out this experiment yourselves, for present company is always excluded when negative assertions are being made—you may have witnessed how the rotation of the planets around the Sun was graphically illustrated even to a class of young children. A piece of cardboard is cut into a disc and its center is pierced with a pin. A drip of oil is then put onto its surface before the disc is floated on water. When the pin is twirled around to rotate the floating disc, little droplets of oil will shoot off at a tangent, making "little planets"—little oil planets—and in this way a most convincing model of a planetary system has been fabricated. Needless to say, this experiment is supposed to prove the accuracy of the Kant-Laplace theory. Well, as far as one's own morality is concerned, it is virtuous enough to be self-effacing, but in a scientific experiment of this sort, the first requirement is certainly not to omit any essential detail—however small—and to include all existing criteria. And isn't the teacher spinning the disc the most important factor involved? Therefore, this hypothesis would make sense only if it were assumed that, long, long ago, a gigantic schoolmaster once twirled round an immense world-pin, thus spinning our entire planetary system! Otherwise one should not use such a hypothetical experiment.

And so, many elements of an unrealistic soul attitude can be detected where science appears to be most correct, where its findings cannot be contested. Consequently these elements of error easily creep into education. For those who teach are inevitably a product of their own time, and this is as it should be. When they come across such geological calculations or astronomical analogies, everything seems to fit together very nicely. Sometimes one cannot help but feel amazed at the incredible ingenuity of scientific interpretations that, despite their apparent power of conviction, nevertheless, can lead us away from reality. However, as educators we must never deviate from actual reality. In teaching, we face reality all the time, and this must spur us on to greater knowledge of human nature as it really is. In a certain sense this failure to penetrate human nature has already crept into modern-day educational thinking and practice.

I would like to illustrate this point with an example. Whenever you are dealing with children in the classroom, you will find that some are more gifted in one or another subject than others. Most of you will be familiar with the current thoughts and methods regarding this problem. I am referring to them here only to establish mutual understanding. There are different degrees of abilities in children. And how are these dealt with, especially in today's most progressive centers for educational science? From your study of educational literature you probably know about the so-called correlation coefficients recently introduced in schools. According to this method, the correlation coefficient *one* is written down if a pupil shows an equal aptitude for two different subjects. (Such a thing actually never occurs, but hypothetically it is simply assumed.) If, on the other hand, a natural gift exists for two subjects that are mutually incompatible, the correlation coefficient *zero* is given. The idea of this method is to test and measure the pupils' various gifts. For example, you may find that drawing and writing carry the correlation coefficient of, let us say, .7. This means that more than half the children who are gifted in drawing also have a natural skill for writing. One also looks for correlation coefficients in other combinations of talents. For example, writing is linked to a pupil's ability to deal with the mother tongue and, in this case, the correlation coefficient is .54. Arithmetic and writing carry the correlation coefficient of .2, arithmetic and drawing .19, and so on. From this it can be seen that arithmetic and drawing are the least compatible partners, whereas writing and drawing are matched most frequently. A natural gift for both the mother tongue and for drawing is found to be equally present in approximately fifty percent of the pupils.

Please note that, on principle, I do not object to this kind of scientific research. It would be wrong to declare that such things should not be investigated. As a matter of fact, I find these things extraordinarily interesting. I am not in the least against such experimental or statistical methods of psychology.

But if their results are directly implemented in education, it is as if you were to ask someone to become a painter without mentioning the importance of having to deal with color. It is as if one were to say instead to such a person, "Look, here is a good book on esthetics. Read the chapter about painting and, in itself, that will make you into a good painter."

A well-known painter in Munich once told me a story that I have quoted several times. While he was a student at the local arts school, Carriere,[3] the famous professor of esthetics, was lecturing in Munich. One day the painter and some of his fellow students decided to go and see this famous expert who also lectured on painting. But one visit was enough for them, because, as they put it, all he did was "crow with esthetic delight."

This is how it strikes me if people think they can benefit their educational practice with the kind of thing mentioned above. Though these experiments may be interesting from a scientific perspective, something very different is needed for the practical classroom situation. It is necessary, for example, that teachers can penetrate human nature so deeply that they can recognize the origin of the skills for drawing and writing within the inner functions, or recognize what enables a pupil to speak the mother tongue well. To achieve such a faculty, a living observation of the human being is required, which eventually may lead one to discover how specific capacities flow out of some children for, let us say, drawing or the skill for their native language. Here, statistics are of little use. One must take a cue from what children reveal of themselves. At most, such statistical evidence may serve as an interesting confirmation afterward. Statistics do have their value, but to believe that they are tools for educational practice only shows the degree of one's alienation from real human nature.

---

3. Moritz Carriere (1817–1895) German thinker; published *Aesthetics* in 1815.

Today, many people look at statistics as a key to understanding human beings. In certain areas of life this is justified. It is possible to build a statistical picture of the human being, but such a picture will not allow us to understand the human being in depth. Think, for instance, of how useful statistics are in their appropriate sphere, such as in insurance. If I want to take out a life insurance policy, I will be asked how old I am, and I must give evidence for the state of my health, and so on. From such data the level of my premium can be worked out very neatly, depending on whether I happen to be a youngster or an old fogy. My life expectancy is then calculated and these details meet exactly the needs of the insurance business. But what if, in my thirty-seventh year, I had taken out a life insurance policy for, let us say, twenty years? Would this make me feel obliged to die at the age of fifty-seven, simply because of what was calculated on paper? To enter fully into the stream of life is something very different from following certain established criteria, however logically correct they may be, or however beneficial they may be in their proper sphere.

When considering the question of aptitude for writing and drawing in children who have recently entered school, one must remember that they have reached the stage of their second dentition. In the coming lectures you will hear more about the different stages of children's development, and about how their ages can be divided into three groups: the period from birth to the change of teeth; from the second dentition to puberty; and the time following puberty. Later we shall go into more detail about what happens in children during these three periods.

For now let us consider this question of writing and drawing. Science, having scrutinized so minutely the three kingdoms of nature that surround us, now transfers the knowledge gained to the human being. Knowledge of the outer world and the mode of thinking about outer nature now becomes the key to understanding the human individual. And yet, if one observes the human being within the human sphere, one will come to recognize the true situation. One only needs the courage to do so with the same accuracy and objectivity used to study outer nature. Current research shows such courage only when observing external nature, but shrinks from applying the same methods in the study of the human being.

Let's look at how the child develops from birth to the change of teeth. This change of teeth is a unique event in life, inasmuch as it occurs only once in life. Now, if you can experience something similar to the feelings Tagore expressed when he saw the amputated leg, you will realize that what is revealed in the change of teeth does not just happen in the jaws, but encompasses the entire human being. You will feel that something must be pervading the whole child until around the age of seven, and that some activity must reach a climax in the change of teeth. This activity is there in its original form until the seventh year, and then it is no longer present in its original state.

When studying physics, for example, scientists have the courage to speak of *latent heat* as distinct from the various forms of *liberated heat*. According to this concept, there must be some form of heat that cannot be determined with a thermometer, but can be measured after it has been released. When characterizing these phenomena that occur in nature, scientists have shown courage in their interpretations. However, when the human being becomes the object of study, this courage is no longer there. Otherwise they would not hesitate to state: What has been working until the seventh year in the child, working toward liberation during the change of teeth, must have been connected with the physical organism before becoming freed and reappearing in a different guise as the child's inner soul properties. This same process can also be recognized in other areas of the child's bone formation. One would realize that these newly emerging powers must be the same, although transformed, as what had been active previously in the child's physical organism.

Only courage is needed to look at the human being with the same cognitive powers used to study outer nature, but modern science will not do this. However, if we do this, our attention is drawn toward all that belongs to the bony system, to everything that hardens the human form to give it structure and support. Orthodox physiology might eventually go this far—if not today, then certainly in due time. The most important branches of science are going through considerable changes just now, and the time will come when they will follow the course indicated.

But something else must also be considered. In later years, the child will be introduced to many different subjects, such as geometry. In today's intellectual age, one has an abstract concept of three-dimensional space, to choose a very simple example. One imagines:

three lines at right angles to one another hovering about in space and extending to infinity. It is possible to form such a concept abstractly, but in such a case it is not inwardly experienced. And yet, three-dimensional space wants to be experienced as reality. This does happen in a young child, although unconsciously, at the crawling stage when, losing its balance time and again, it will eventually learn to acquire the upright position and achieve equilibrium in the world. Here we have a case of actual experience of three-dimensional space. This is not merely a question of drawing three lines in space, because one of these three dimensions is identical with the human upright position (which we can test by no longer assuming it— that is, by lying horizontally or sleeping). This upright position signals the most fundamental difference between the human being and the animal, because, unlike the human backbone, the animal's spinal column runs parallel to Earth's surface. We experience the second dimension unconsciously every time we stretch our arms sideways. The third dimension moves from our front toward the back.

In reality these three dimensions are experienced concretely as above and below, right and left, forward and backward. What is done in geometry is merely an abstraction. Human beings do experience with their bodies what is shown in geometrical constructions, but only during the age when they are still largely unconscious and dreamy. Later on, these experiences rise into consciousness and assume abstract forms.

With the change of teeth, the forces that cause an inner firmness, an inner consolidation and support, have reached a certain climax. From the moment when the child can stand upright until the inner hardening processes manifest in the change of teeth, the child inwardly tries, although unconsciously, "body geometry" as an activity akin to drawing. When the teeth change, this becomes a soul activity—that is, it enters the realm of the child's soul. We might understand this transformation better through an analogy; just as a sediment falls to the bottom when a chemical solution cools, and leaves the upper part clearer, so there is also a physiological aspect to the hardening process—the sediment, as well as its counterpart: the clear solution within the child's soul realm, which manifests as a faculty for *geometrizing*, for drawing, and so on.

After this period, we can see the child's soul qualities streaming outward. Just think about how such a discovery engenders real interest in the human being. We shall observe this streaming out in greater detail, and how it is reflected back again, later on.

In this respect everything in life is linked together. What we do to the child not only has an immediate effect, but influences the whole lifetime. Only a few people are prepared to observe a human life as a whole, but most focus their attention on present circumstances only. This is the case, for example, when one creates an experiment concerned only with the present. On the other hand, have you ever observed how the mere presence of some old people can be like a blessing for the others present? They need not even say a word. Goodness radiates from their presence simply through what they have become. And if you now search the biography of such old people, you may find that when they were children they learned to feel reverence quite naturally, without any outer compulsion. I could say equally that they learned how to pray, by which I mean praying in its widest sense, which includes a deep respect and admiration for another human being. I would like to express this thought in the form of a picture. Those who have not learned to fold their hands in prayer during childhood, cannot spread them in blessing in old age.

The different phases of life are all interconnected and it is of great importance in education to take this into full account. We learn a great deal about the child when we recognize how soul forces well forth after they have completed their task of working in the physical body up to the end of the first seven-year period.

Psychologists have made the strangest hypotheses about the interplay of soul and body, whereas one period of life actually sheds light on another. What we can see in the child between the change of teeth and puberty will tell us something about the soul forces previously engaged in working within the child's physical realm. Facts speak for themselves and shed light on one another. Think of how such things will stimulate interest in education! And genuine interest in the human being is needed in education today. Far too many people think about the relationship of body and soul—or of soul and body—only in abstract terms. And because so little of real value has emerged, a rather amusing theory has been formulated—that is, the theory of the so-called *psycho-physical parallelism*. According to this theory, processes of soul and body run side by side on a parallel course. There is no need to bother about points of intersection, no need to bother about the relationship between body and soul at all, because they supposedly meet at infinity! That is why this theory sounds like a joke.

However, if one allows the guidance of practical experience, one can discover the actual interrelationship between body and soul. One only needs to look over a person's whole life-span. Let us take the example of someone who develops diabetes or rheumatism at a certain age. When trying to find a remedy for such an illness, usually only the present conditions are considered; this, in itself, is quite justified. It is certainly proper to make every effort to heal a sickness whenever it occurs. But if one surveys the whole life of the patient, one may discover that many times diabetes is due to a memory that was overtaxed or developed in the wrong way between the change of teeth and puberty. Health during later years is largely conditioned by the way a person's soul life was developed during childhood. The way a child's memory is trained will affect the metabolism after a certain period of time. For example, if undigested vestiges of memory remain in the soul of a child between seven and fourteen, they will be released approximately between the ages of thirty-five and forty-five as physical residues, which can then lead to rheumatism or diabetes.

It is not an understatement to suggest that teachers should have at least a modicum of medical knowledge at their disposal. It is not right for them to leave everything concerning the child's health to the school doctor, who usually doesn't even know the children. If any profession in our time requires a wider background, education needs it most of all.

This is what I wanted to tell you as an introduction to our conference theme, so that you can judge for yourselves when you hear people say that anthroposophy now dabbles also in education, whereas others believe that it has something valid to say on the subject. Those who are ready to listen will not be swayed by those who have the opinion that there is no real need for education, or that there is no point in discussing it simply because their own experiences in this area have been so frustrating. Anthroposophy begins with an entirely different attitude. It does not simply want to correct old ideas, but begins with a true picture and knowledge of the human being, because, in keeping with human progress, these things have become necessary today.

If you go back to the earlier forms of education, you will discover that they have all arisen from the general culture of their time, from the universal nature of human feelings and experiences. We must rediscover a universal approach, flowing from human nature itself. If I had my way, I would give anthroposophy a new name every day to prevent people from hanging on to its literal meaning, from translating it from the Greek, so they can form judgments accordingly. It is immaterial what name we attach to what is being done here. The only thing that matters is that everything we do here is focused on life's realities and that we never lose sight of them. We must never be tempted to implement sectarian ideas.

And so, looking at education in general, we encounter the opinion that there are already plenty of well-considered educational systems; but since we are all suffering so much from the intellectualism of our times, it would be best if the intellect were banished from education. This is very correct, but then it is concluded that, instead of developing a science of education, again we should appeal to our inherent pedagogical instincts. However desirable this may sound, it is no longer possible today because humankind has moved to a further stage of development. The healthy instincts of the past are no longer with us today. A new and unbiased look at education has to be backed by fully conscious cognition, and this is possible only if our understanding can penetrate the very nature of the human being. This is what anthroposophy is all about.

One more point: intellectualism and abstractions are rampant today to the degree where there is a general feeling that children should be protected from an education that is too intellectual, that their hearts and feelings should also be educated. This is entirely correct, but when looking into educational literature and current practice, one cannot help noticing that such good intentions are not likely to go very far because, once again, they are formulated in a theoretical and abstract way. It is even less clear that this request should be made, not just on behalf of the child, but should be addressed also to the teachers and, most of all, to the pedagogical principles themselves. To do this is my goal. We must not give mere lip service when stating how we wish to educate the heart of the child and not just the intellect, but we should ask ourselves how we can best meet this challenge. What do we have to do so that education can have a heart again?

Lecture Two

DORNACH, APRIL 16, 1923

To begin with we will try to understand more fully the nature of the growing human being, bearing in mind the later stages in life, in order to draw conclusions about education from our findings. Knowledge of the human being made possible through anthroposophical research—as outlined briefly yesterday—fundamentally differs from the findings of modern science and other research. The knowledge of the human being produced by our contemporary civilization is based mainly on what remains when the human spirit and part of the human soul are ignored. Such knowledge rests on what can be found, both anatomically and physiologically, when one looks at a corpse. Furthermore, it is supported by investigations into pathological changes, due to illness or other causes, from which conclusions are drawn with regard to the healthy human being. What is gained through this approach then forms the background for the attitude from which judgments are made regarding the living, healthy human being.

The anthroposophical approach begins by looking at the human being as an entity, an organization of body, soul, and spirit. It attempts to comprehend the human being not in an abstract and dead way, but through a living mode of observation that can recognize and comprehend with living concepts the human totality of spirit, soul, and body. This approach enables us to perceive accurately the various metamorphoses that take place during a lifetime. Children are different beings depending on whether they are going through the development between birth and change of teeth, or between the second dentition and puberty—the latter period being the time when they are in the care of the class teacher—or during the stage following puberty. Human beings are completely different creatures depending on which of these three stages they are going through. But the differences are so deeply hidden that they escape a more external form of observation. This external method of observation does not lead to a clear perception and judgment of how body, soul, and spirit are permeated by spirit in entirely different ways during each of the first three periods of life.

It would surely not be proper for teachers to first acquire theoretical knowledge and then to think: What I have learned in theory I will now apply in my teaching in one way or another. With this attitude they would only distance themselves from the child's true being. Teachers need to transform their knowledge of the human being into a kind of higher instinct whereby they can respond properly to whatever comes from each individual child. This is another way that anthroposophical knowledge of the human being differs from the usual kind, and can lead to a routine approach to education at best, but not to a firmly founded pedagogical sense and teaching practice. To achieve this, one's knowledge of human nature must be capable of becoming pedagogical instinct the moment one has to deal with a child, so that in response to all that comes from the child one knows instantly and exactly what must be done in every single case. If I may use a comparison, there are all kinds of theories about what we should eat or drink, but in ordinary life we do not usually follow such theoretical directions. We drink when thirsty and eat when hungry, according to the constitution of the human organism. Eating and drinking follow a certain rhythmical pattern for good reasons, but usually one eats and drinks when hungry or thirsty; life itself sees to that.

Knowledge of the human being, which forms the basis of a sound and practical way of teaching, must create in the teachers, every time they face a child, something like the relationship between hunger and eating. The teachers' response to a given pedagogical situation has to become as natural as satisfying a sensation of hunger by eating. This is only possible if knowledge of the human being has permeated flesh and blood as well as soul and spirit, so that you intuitively know what needs to be done every time you face a child. Only if your knowledge of human beings has such inner fullness that it can become instinctive can it lead to the proper kind of practical teaching. It will not happen on the basis of psychological experiments leading to theories about pupils' powers of memory, concentration, and so on. In that case, intellectual ideas are inserted between theory and practice. This presents an unreal situation that externalizes all educational methods and practice. The first thing to be aimed for is a living comprehension of the child in all its pulsing life.

Let's look now at young children as they grow into earthly life. Let our observations be straightforward and simple, and we shall find that there are three things with which they have to come to terms, three activities that become a decisive factor for the entire life to come. These are what are simply called walking, speaking, and thinking.

Jean Paul—this is the name he gave himself—once said: "The human being learns more for the whole of life during the first three years than he does during his three years at university."[1] This is entirely true; it is a fact. For even if academic

---

1. Jean Paul (Friedrich Richter) (1763–1825) German poet.

studies nowadays extend over longer periods of time, their gain for life amounts to less than what is acquired for the whole of life during the time when children are learning how to walk, speak, and think.

What does it actually mean when we say the child is learning to walk, speak, and think? The capacity to walk comprises far more than is generally realized. It is by no means simply a case of the young child—after the stage of crawling—managing to stand up and take the first steps in order to develop what will eventually become an individual and characteristic way of walking. An inner adjustment underlies learning to walk; there is an inner orientation of the young child. The equilibrium of the organism, with all its possibilities for movement, becomes related to the equilibrium and all the possibilities for movement of the whole universe, because the child stands within it. While learning to walk, children are seeking to relate their own equilibrium to that of the entire cosmos.

They are also seeking the specifically human relationship between the activities of arms and hands and those of the lower limbs. The movements of arms and hands have a special affinity to the life of the soul, while those of the legs lag behind, serving more the physical body. This is of immense importance for the whole of later life. The differentiation between the activities of legs and feet and those of arms and hands represents the human quest for balance of soul that is lifelong.

When raising themselves up, young children are first of all seeking physical balance. But when freely moving arms and hands, they are also seeking balance of soul. There is infinitely more than meets the eye hidden behind what is commonly called "learning to walk," as everyone can find out. The expression "learning to walk" signifies only the most obvious and outwardly important aspect perceptible to our senses. A deeper look at this phenomenon would make one wish to characterize it in the following way. To learn to walk is to learn to experience the principles of statics and dynamics in one's own inner being and to relate these to the entire universe.[2] Better still, to learn to walk is to meet the forces of statics and dynamics both in body and soul and to relate these experiences to the whole cosmos. This is what learning to walk is all about. But through the fact that the movements of arms and hands have become emancipated from those of the legs and feet, something else has happened. A basis has been created for attaining a purely human development. Thus, the child who is learning to walk adapts itself outwardly to the external, visible world with its own rhythms and beat, as well as inwardly with its entire inner being.

So you see that something very noteworthy is woven into the development of the human being. The activities of the legs, in a certain way, have the effect of producing in the physical and soul life a stronger connection with what is of the nature of beat, of what cuts into life. In the characteristic attunement of the movements of right and left leg, we learn to relate ourselves to what lies below our feet. And then, through the emancipation of the movements of our arms from those of our legs, a new musical and melodious element is introduced into the beat and rhythm provided by the activities of our legs. The content of our lives—or one might say, the themes of our lives—comes to the fore in the movements of our arms. Their activity, in turn, forms the basis for what is being developed when the child is learning to speak. Outwardly, this is already shown through the fact that with most people, the stronger activity of

---

2. The terms *statics* and *dynamics*, the principles of rest or equilibrium and of movement, are used by Steiner in various ways in this and the following lectures. These polar forces, active in the young child, work in full coordination in walking, while the body's weight is being transferred from one leg to the other. The way that a child gradually learns to control these forces is not only highly individual, but is significant for the child's entire life. — TRANS.

the right arm corresponds to the formation of the left speech organ. From the relationship between the activities of legs and arms, as you can observe them in a freely moving human being, yet another relationship comes into being. It is the relationship that the child gains to the surrounding world through learning to speak.

When you look at how all this is interconnected and belongs together, when you see how in the process of sentence formation the legs are working upwards into speech, and how the content, the meaning of words, enters into the process of sound production—that is, into the inner experience of the structure of the sentences—you have an impression of how the beat-like, rhythmical element of the moving legs works upon the more musical-thematic and inward element of the moving arms and hands. Consequently, if a child walks with firm and even steps, if its walk does not tend to be slovenly, you have the physical basis—which, naturally, is a manifestation of the spirit, as we shall see later—for a good feeling for the structure of both spoken and written sentences. Through the movement of the legs, the child learns to form correct sentences. You will also find that if a child has a slouching gait, it will have difficulties finding the right intervals between sentences, and that the contours of its sentences become blurred. Likewise, if a child does not learn to move its arms harmoniously, its speech will become rasping and unmelodious.[3] In addition, if you cannot help a child to become sensitive in its fingertips, it will not develop the right sense for modulation in speech.

All this refers to the time when the child learns to walk and talk. But something else can also be detected. You may have noticed that in life the proper timing of certain processes is

---

3. The German word *Intervall* refers to differences in pitch only, and not to a break in the flow of time. — TRANS.

sometimes disturbed, that certain phases of development make their appearance later than one would expect according to the natural course of development. But in this context you can also see that the proper sequence of events can be safeguarded if children are encouraged to learn to walk first, that is, if one can possibly avoid having children learn to speak before they can walk. Speech has to be developed on the basis of the right kind of walking and of the free movement of the arms. Otherwise, children's speech will not be anchored in their whole being. Instead, they will only babble indistinctly. You may have come across some people whose speech sounded not unlike bleating. In such a case, not enough attention was paid to what I have just tried to characterize.

The third faculty the child must learn on the basis of walking and speaking is thinking, which should gradually become more and more conscious. But this faculty ought to be developed last, for it lies in the child's nature to learn to think only through speaking. In its early stages, speaking is an imitation of the sounds that the child hears. As the sounds are perceived by the child in whom the characteristic relationship between the movements of the legs and arms is deeply rooted, it learns intuitively to make sense of the sounds that it imitates, though without linking any thought to what it has heard. At first, the child only links feelings to the sounds coming toward it. Thinking, which arises later, can develop only out of speech. Therefore, the correct sequence we need to encourage in the growing child is learning to walk, learning to speak, and finally, learning to think.

We must now enter a bit more deeply into these three important processes of development. Thinking, which is—or ought to be—the last faculty developed, always has the quality of mirroring, or reflecting, outer nature and its processes. Moral impulses do not originate in the sphere of thinking, as we all know. They arise in that part of the human being we call the conscience, about which we shall have more to say later on. In any case, human conscience arises in the depths of the soul before penetrating the sphere of thinking. The faculty of thinking, on the other hand, that we acquire in childhood, is attuned only to perceiving the essence of outer nature and its processes. Thus all of the child's first thinking is aimed at creating images of outer nature and its processes.

However, when we turn to learning to speak, we come across quite a different situation. With regard to the development of this faculty, present-day science has been able to make only tentative observations. Orthodox science has achieved quite wonderful results, for instance in its investigations into the animal world. And when it compares its findings with what happens in a human being, it has made many discoveries that deserve our full recognition. But with regard to the comprehension of the processes taking place when a child is learning to speak, contemporary science has remained rather in the dark.

The same applies to animal communication through sound. And here a key question needs to be answered first. In order to speak, the human being uses the larynx and other speech organs. The higher animals also possess these organs, even if in a more primitive form. If we disregard certain animals capable of producing sounds that in some species have developed into a kind of singing, but think instead of animals that emit only very primitive sounds, an obvious question comes to mind (and I raise this question not only from a causal, but also from quite a utilitarian point of view). Why should such animals have a larynx with its neighboring organs, since these are used for speech only by the human being? Though the animal is not capable of using them for speaking, they are there nevertheless, and this even very markedly. Comparative anatomy shows that even in relatively dumb animals—dumb in comparison with the human being—organs of this kind exist.

It is a fact that these organs, at least to a certain extent, have possibilities destined to be realized only by the human being. Though incapable of making use of these organs for speech, the animal nevertheless possesses them. What is the meaning of this? A more advanced physiology will come to discover that the animal forms of the various species depend, in each case, upon the animal's larynx and its neighboring organs. If, for instance, a certain animal grows into a lion, the underlying causes have to be looked for in its upper chest organs. From there, forces are radiating out that create the form of a lion. If an animal grows into a cow, the cause of this particular form is to be found in what becomes the speech organ in the human being. From these organs, the forces creating the animal forms radiate. One day this will have to be studied in detail in order to learn how to approach morphology more realistically. Then one will find out how to correctly study animal forms, how to grasp the nature of the upper chest organs and the way these pass over into the organs of the mouth. For it is from this region that forces radiate creating the entire animal form.

Human beings form these organs into speech organs on the basis of their upright walk and freely moving arms. They take in what works through sound and speech from their surroundings—if we are dealing with present times. And what is it they absorb in this way? Think of how the potential to give form to the entire human organism lies in these organs. This means that if, for instance, a child hears an angry or passionate voice, if it is surrounded by loud and ill-tempered shouting, it will absorb something the animal keeps out. The animal lets itself be shaped only by the larynx and its neighboring organs, but members of the human species allow vehement or passionate voices to enter their inner being. These sounds flow into the human form, right into the structure of the most delicate tissues. If children hear only gentle speech in their surroundings, this too flows right into the structure of their finest tissues. It flows into their very formation, and especially so into the more refined parts of their organization. The coarser parts are able to withstand these influences, as in the case of the animal. But whatever is taken in through speech flows into the finer parts of the child's organization. This is how the differing organizations of the various nations come about. They all flow out of the language spoken. The human being is an imprint of language. You will therefore be able to appreciate what it means that in the course of human evolution so many people have learned to speak several languages. It has had the effect of making such people more universal. These things are of immense importance for human development.

And so we see how during the early period of childhood the human being is inwardly predisposed, right down to the blood circulation, by what comes from the environment. These influences become instrumental for the orientation of a person's thought life. What happens in a human being through learning to speak is something I ask you to consider most seriously. This human faculty might best be understood in its essence by comparing it with animal development. If an animal could express what lives in its forming and shaping, emanating from its upper chest organs, it would have to say, My form conforms with what streams from my upper chest and mouth organs, and I do not allow anything to enter my being that would modify this form. So would the animal speak if it were able to express this relationship. The human being, on the other hand, would say, I adapt the upper organs of my chest and mouth to the world processes that work through language, and I adjust the structure of my innermost organization accordingly.

The human being adapts the most inward physical organization to what comes from the surroundings through language, but not the outer organization, which develops in a

way similar to that of animals. This is of immense importance
for an understanding of the entire human being. For out of
language, the general orientation of thought is developed, and
because of this the human being during the first three years of
life is given over entirely to what comes from the outer world,
whereas the animal is rigidly enclosed within itself. Accordingly, the way that we find our relationship during these three
years to statics and dynamics, then to speech, and finally to
thinking, is of such profound importance. It is essential that
this process develops in the right way. No doubt you are all
aware that this can happen in the most varied ways in each
individual human being.

Whether these processes take their proper course depends on
many things. But the most fundamental factor during the first
stage of childhood is the right relationship between the child's
times of sleeping and waking. This means that we have to
acquire an instinctive knowledge of how much sleep a child
needs and how long it should be awake. For example, suppose
that a child sleeps too much, relatively speaking. In this case it
will develop a tendency to hold back in the activity of its legs. If
a child gets too much sleep, inwardly it will lose the will to walk.
It will become lethargic in its walking, and, because of this, it
will also become lazy in its speech. Such a child will not develop
a proper flow in its speech and it will speak more slowly than it
should according to its natural disposition. When we meet such
a person in later life—unless this imbalance has been put right
during the subsequent school years—we sometimes despair
because he or she gives us the opportunity, one might say, to go
for a little walk between every two words spoken. There are such
people who have difficulties in finding their way from one word
to the next. And if we come across them and look at their childhood, we will find that when they were learning to walk, they
were allowed to sleep too much.

too much sleep early childhood.

Now let us take the case of a child whose parents or those in charge did not ensure that it had the relatively long hours of sleep appropriate to its age. The inner being of such a child is incapable of gaining the necessary control over its leg movements. Instead of walking normally, the child will have a floppy gait. In its speech, instead of controlling the sequential flow of words with the forces of the soul, it will let the words fall out of its mouth. The words of the sentences will not cohere. This is quite different from the case of a child who has difficulties in finding the right words. Here an overabundance of speech energy prevents it from getting from one word on to the next. Thus, in the instance mentioned previously, I was referring to the opposite, namely to a lack of the necessary energy. The words, as they follow each other, are not carried along by the flow of the soul; instead, the child waits for the right moment to "click in" the next word. If this reaches extreme proportions, the result is stammering. If one finds a tendency toward stammering in people, especially in their twenties and thirties, one can be sure that as young children they were not given enough sleep. From this you can see how knowledge of the human being can give us the fundamentals of what needs to be done.

Now let us consider the entire human organism and see how during the first three years it adapts itself to earthly conditions of life, how it allows the principles of statics and dynamics, underlying the faculty of autonomous movement, to flow into what is produced through shaping the air in speech. In this process there is much more involved that is of consequence for the development of thinking. Compare this situation with that of an adult, and you will see that in the child there is a much stronger working together of these inner dynamics—of walking, fidgeting, movements of arms, and creating mental images. In the child all this flows together into a unity far more than in the adult.

The child remains a far more homogeneous being than a grown-up in other respects as well. If, for instance, we as adults suck a sweet (which we really shouldn't do), this merely amounts to a titillation of the tongue, for the sweet taste does not go much further than that. But the child is in a different position. There the taste continues to spread. Children don't tell us this and we don't notice it; nevertheless, the taste continues to have an effect upon the child. Many among you will surely have observed how, according to their individual makeup, certain children are strongly permeated by soul and spiritual forces and how this quality comes to outer expression in them. It is far more interesting to watch the arms and legs of such a lively child than its mouth, when it is standing some distance away from a table where there is a bowl full of sugar. What the mouth says is more or less obvious, but the way such a child develops desire right down to its toes, or in the arms, as it steers toward the sugar bowl: you can clearly see it is not just a matter of the tongue anticipating sweetness, but changes are taking place throughout the entire being of the child. Here, tasting flows throughout the whole human being. If you enter into these things without preconceptions, you will come to realize that the young child, in a certain sense, is really just one great sense organ. Mainly this is so during the very first years (and more generally so between birth and the change of teeth) and is, naturally, less so in later years. What has become localized in the sense organs on the periphery of the human body in the adult, permeates the child's entire organism.

Of course, you must understand these things with a certain discernment, but fundamentally they are real. Their existence is so real that orthodox physiology will one day be able to prove them with regard to the most conspicuous of all our sense organs, namely the human eye. People come to me quite frequently and ask, Considering the present state of science, what would you recommend as a suitable theme for a thesis? (Theses, too, belong to the chapter on "school misery.") If such a question is asked by students of physiology, I refer them to a topical problem. I tell them to observe the developmental phases of the human eye as seen in the embryo, and then to compare these with the corresponding phases of the entire embryo from its germinal stage onward. This will lead them to a kind of inverted parallel between the eye and the whole embryo as its development progresses. They will discover that, in a certain way, the eye begins its development later, it omits the first stages. In contrast, the embryo as an entity never reaches its final stage—as the eye does—but stops short beforehand. This points to something of great significance for embryology. If one looks at the whole development of the embryo, one will come to recognize that in these beginning stages we may observe ideal stages that exist only as an indication. The eye continues to develop into a perfected sense organ, whereas the embryo remains behind in its development only to continue its further growth later on.

But the situation in the young child is still one where, in its entire soul and spiritual development, the child's senses are poured out, as it were, over all of its corporeality. In a certain way the child is entirely a sense organ and it confronts the world as such. This has to be borne in mind, not only with regard to educational matters, but concerning everything that is happening in the child's environment before the change of teeth. We shall go into questions relating to more practical methods of teaching at a later stage. But it is only if one can see the fundamentals in the right light that one will be able to find the correct answers to particular human questions. One of these has been handed to me, which is of extraordinary importance for anyone who does not merely look at human evolution from external and well-known aspects of history.

In the past, as you know, there was far more discussion of sin and original sin than is customary today. Now I do not wish to go into this question in detail, I only want to outline what this expression implied to those who studied such questions as we study general scientific subjects today (not in its present popular sense where such matters have undergone a certain coarsening). To those enquiring minds, original sin stood for *all inherited* characteristics.[4] This means that what a person had inherited from his or her forebears was considered to represent original sin. Such was the actual concept of this expression; only later on was it changed to what we associate it with today. In earlier times, it was definitely felt that physical features inherited from one's ancestors gave rise to sinfulness.

And what do we say today? We not only believe in studying inherited characteristics most carefully, but we even encourage their cultivation! If an earlier form of science had been asked to judge the modern attitude, it would have responded, With all your progress you have managed to come up with a most extraordinary principle—you have actually taught society to cultivate what is of sinful origin in the human being! Because we know of historical events only from what is rather superficially recorded in history books, we do not notice such subtle changes of interpretation.

If you look into what I have told you today—namely how the child, through its relationship to dynamics and statics, through learning to speak and to think, adapts itself to the environment—then you will be able to distinguish between the part played by purely physical heredity and that of the environmental influences, which are far stronger than is generally realized. Often we hear it said that someone has inherited a particular

---

4. The German word for "original sin" is *Erbsunde,* which means literally "inherited sin." — TRANS.

trait from either the father or the mother, whereas in reality it is simply the result of imitating a certain way of walking, or a characteristic gesture of hands, or a specific manner of speaking, from those close to the person in his or her early childhood. The child's total surrender to the influences of the environment is what is of pre-eminent importance during the first years and not heredity as such. In their proper place, theories of heredity have their justification, but these also need to be seen within the context of what I said yesterday, when speaking about soft ground into which footmarks were imprinted.

If now some hypothetical Martian were to appear on the Earth, a being unacquainted with the human race, it might explain the origin of these footprints in the following way: Certain forces have pushed up the Earth, more in some places and less in others, which has caused the configuration of these footmarks. This is how some people would explain the nature of the human soul on the basis of heredity and as a result of the working of the brain. Just as the footprints have been pressed into the Earth from outside, so have environmental influences, experienced during the childhood stage of imitation, through learning to walk, speak, and think, been imprinted in the body, and particularly so in the brain and the nervous system.

What orthodox physical psychology maintains is perfectly correct. The brain is a clear imprint of what the human individual is as a being of soul. One only has to know that the brain is not the cause, the creator of the soul element, but the ground on which the soul develops. Just as I cannot walk without the ground under my feet, neither can I, as a physical being, think without a brain. This is obvious. But the brain is no more than the ground into which the activities of thinking and speaking imprint what is received from the surrounding world. It is not a matter of heredity.

Perhaps now you can see that people tend to have only unclear notions about what is happening in the child during these first three "nonacademic" years. During that time, to a large extent, the foundations are being laid for a person's whole inner life and configuration. I have already spoken of how thinking, which develops later, turns toward the outer world. It forms images of the natural world and its processes. But the faculty of speaking, which is developed earlier, absorbs—at least in nuances and in modified form—what lives spiritually in language. And language, coming from the child's environment, works upon the child's soul. Through language we take in from our surroundings what we make our own in the realm of the soul. The entire soul atmosphere of our surroundings permeates us through the medium of language. And we know that the child is one great sense organ; we know that inner processes are inaugurated through these soul impressions.

If a child, for example, is frequently exposed to the outbursts of an over-choleric father who utters his words as if in constant anger, it will inwardly experience its father's entire soul background through the way he forms his words. And this has an effect not only on the child's soul, but, through the atmosphere of anger surrounding it, causes the activity of fine glandular secretions to increase as well. Eventually, the glands of such a child become accustomed to an enhanced activity of secretion, and this can affect the whole life of such a child. Unless these harmful influences are balanced through the right kind of education later on, a tendency will develop toward nervous anxieties in any angry atmosphere. Here you have an example of how a certain soul condition directly enters and affects the physical organization. The attempt is often made to comprehend the relationship between the human soul and body, but a fact such as this, where during the first period of life a physical condition directly manifests itself as a symptom in the realm of the soul, simply goes unnoticed.

While the child enters into the realm of statics and dynamics working through its surroundings, it does something unconsciously that is of great importance. Think for a moment of how much trouble it means for many an older pupil to learn the laws of statics and dynamics and to apply them, even if only in the field of mechanics. The young child does this unconsciously. It incorporates statics and dynamics into its entire being. Anthroposophical research shows us that what most accomplished experts in the field of statics and dynamics manage to think out for the external world is child's play compared with the way the child incorporates these complicated forces while learning to walk. It does so through imitation. Here is an opportunity to observe the strange outer effects of imitation in just this situation. You can find many examples in life. I will give you one.

There once were two girls of roughly the same age, who could be seen walking side by side. This case happened many years ago, in a town in central Germany. When they walked next to each other, they both limped with one leg. While both were performing the same limb movements, they displayed a marked difference between the movements of their more mobile right arms and right fingers and a somewhat paralyzed way they carried their left arms and left fingers. Both children were exact copies of each other. The slightly younger one was a true copy of the older one. And yet, only the older sister had a damaged left leg. Both legs of the younger one were perfectly normal. It was only by sheer imitation that she copied the movements of her handicapped sister. You can find similar cases everywhere, though many of them, being less conspicuous, may easily escape your notice.

When a child learns to walk, when it makes the principles of statics and dynamics its own, it takes in the spirit in its environment. One could formulate it in this way: In learning to walk, we take hold of the soul element of our milieu. And in what the child ought to learn first after entering earthly life, it takes hold of the spirit in its surroundings.

Spirit, soul, and body—spirit, soul, and nature—this is the right order in which the surrounding world approaches the human being. But as we take hold of the soul element in our surroundings, we also lay the foundations for our future sympathies and antipathies in life. These flow into us quite unnoticed. The way we learn to speak is, at the same time, also the way we acquire certain fundamental sympathies and antipathies. And the most curious aspect of it all is that whoever is able to develop an eye for such matters (an eye of the soul, of course) will find in the way a child walks—whether it does so more with the heel or with the toes, whether it has a firm footstep or whether it creeps along—a preparation for the moral character the child will develop in later life. Thus, we may say that together with the spiritual element the child absorbs while learning to walk, there also flows into it a moral element emanating from the environment. And it is a good thing if one can learn to perceive how the characteristic way a child moves its legs portends its moral character, whether it will develop into a morally good or bad person. For the most naturalistic quality belongs to what we take in through our thinking during childhood. What we absorb through language is already permeated by an element of soul. What we make our own through statics and dynamics is pervaded by moral and spiritual powers. But here statics and dynamics are not of the kind we learn about in school; here they are born directly out of the spirit.

It is most important to look at these matters in the right way, so that one does not arrive at the kind of psychology that is based primarily on physical aspects. In this kind of psychology one reads in fair detail what the author has managed to establish in the first thirty pages of print, only to find that relevant aspects of the soul are stuck on artificially. One must no longer speak today of the human spirit, since an Ecumenical Council abolished it, declaring that the human being does not consist of body, soul and spirit, but only of body and soul, the latter having certain spiritual properties.[5]

The trichotomy of the human being was dogmatically forbidden during the Middle Ages, and today, our contemporary "unbiased" science begins its psychology with the declaration that the human being consists of body and soul only. Blissfully unaware of how little "unbiased" its findings are, it is still adhering to medieval dogmatism. The most erudite university professors follow this ancient dogma without having the slightest notion of it. In order to arrive at an accurate picture of the human being, it is essential to recognize all three constituent parts: body, soul, and spirit.

Materialistic minds can grasp only human thinking—and this is their tragedy. Materialism has the least understanding of matter because it cannot see the spirit working through matter. It can only dogmatize—there is only matter and its effects. But it does not know that everywhere matter is permeated with spirit. If one wants to describe materialism, one has to resort to a paradoxical definition. Materialism is the one view of the world that has no understanding of what matter is.

What is important is to know exactly where the borderlines are between the phenomena of body, soul, and spirit, and how one leads over into the other. This is of special importance with regard to the child's development during the first period of life.

---

5. The Eighth Ecumenical Council in Constantinople in A.D. 869.

Lecture Three

Yesterday I pointed out that there is much more involved in learning to walk, speak, and think—the three most important activities of early childhood—than is apparent outwardly. I also indicated that it is impossible to observe the human being completely without distinguishing between what is internal and what is external. When considering the organization of the whole human being, who is made up of body, soul, and spirit, it is especially necessary to develop a refined faculty of discrimination, and this is particularly true in the field of education.

Let us first look at what is very simply called "learning to walk." I have already mentioned that a part of this activity is connected with how the child establishes equilibrium in the surrounding physical world. The entire, lifelong relationship to static and dynamic forces is involved in this activity. Furthermore, we have seen how this seeking, this striving for balance, this differentiation of arm and hand movements from those of the legs and feet, also forms the basis for the child's faculty of speech. And how, arising out of this faculty, the new faculty of thinking is gradually born. However, in this dynamic system of forces that the child takes hold of in learning how to walk, there lives yet something else that is of a

fundamentally different character. I noted this briefly yesterday, but now we must consider it more fully.

You must always bear in mind that, pre-eminently during
the first stage of childhood, but also up to the change of teeth,
the child is one big sense organ. This is what makes children
receptive to everything that comes from their surroundings.
But it also causes them to recreate inwardly everything that is
going on in their environment. One could say—to choose just
one particular sense organ—that a young child is all eye. Just as
the eye receives stimuli from the external world and, in keeping
with its organization, reproduces what is happening there, so
human beings during the first period of life inwardly reproduce
everything that happens around them.

But the child takes in what is thus coming from the environment with a specific, characteristic form of inner experience.
For example, when seeing the father or the mother moving a
hand or an arm, the child will immediately feel an impulse to
make a similar movement. And so, by imitating the movements of others in the immediate environment, the usual irreg-
ular and fidgety movements of the baby gradually become
more purposeful. In this way the child also learns to walk.

But we must not overemphasize the aspect of heredity in the
acquisition of this faculty, because this constant reference to
heredity is merely a fashion in contemporary natural-scientific
circles. Whether a child first puts down the heel or the toes
when walking is also is due to imitating the father, mother, or
anyone else who is close. Whether a child is more inclined to
imitate one parent or the other depends on how close the connection is with the particular person, the affinity "in between
the lines" of life, if I may put it this way. An exceedingly fine
psychological-physiological process is happening here that cannot be recognized by the blunt tools of today's theories of heredity. To express it more pictorially: Just as the finer particles fall

through the meshes of a sieve while the coarser ones are retained, so does the sieve of the modern world-view allow the finer elements of what is actually happening to slip through. In this way only the coarser similarities between child and father, or child and mother, only the "rough and ready" side of life is reckoned with, disregarding life's finer and more subtle points. The teacher and educator, however, need a trained eye for what is specifically human.

Now it would be natural to assume that it must surely be deep love that motivates a child to imitate one particular person. But if one looks at how love is revealed in later life, even in a very loving person, one will come to realize that if one maintains that the child chooses by means of love, then what is actually happening has not been fully appreciated. For in reality, the child chooses to imitate out of an even higher motive than that of love. The child is prompted by what one might, in later life, call religious or pious devotion. Although this may sound paradoxical, it is nevertheless true. The child's entire sentient-physical behavior in imitation flows from a physical yearning to become imbued with feelings found in later life only in deeply religious devotion or during participation in a religious ritual. This soul attitude is strongest during the child's earliest years, and it continues, gradually declining, until the change of teeth. The physical body of a newborn baby is totally permeated by an inner need for deeply religious devotion. What we call love in later life is just a weakened form of this pious and devotional reverence.

It could be said that until the change of teeth the child is fundamentally an imitative being. But the kind of inner experience that pulses through the child's imitation as its very life blood—and here I must ask you not to misunderstand what I am going to say, for sometimes one has to resort to unfamiliar modes of expression to characterize something that has become alien to our culture—this is religion in a physical, bodily guise.

Until the change of teeth, the child lives in a kind of "bodily religion." We must never underestimate the delicate influences (one could also call them imponderable influences) that, only through a child's powers of perception, emanate from the environment, summoning an urge to imitate. We must in no way underestimate this most fundamental and important aspect of the child's early years. Later on we will see the tremendous significance that this has for both the principles and practical methods of education.

When contemporary natural science examines such matters, the methods used appear very crude, to say the least. To illustrate what I mean, I would like to tell you the case of the mathematician horses that, for awhile, caused a sensation in Germany. I have not seen these Dusseldorf horses myself, but I was in a position to carefully observe the horse belonging to Herr von Osten of Berlin, who played such a prominent part in this affair. It was truly amazing to witness how adept his horse was at simple mathematical calculations. The whole thing caused a great sensation and an extensive treatise dealing with this phenomenon was quickly published by a university lecturer, who came to the following conclusion.

This horse possesses such an unusually fine sensibility that it can perceive the slightest facial expressions of its master, Herr von Osten, as he stands next to it. These facial expressions are so fine that even a human being could not detect them. And when Herr von Osten gives his horse an arithmetical task, he naturally knows the answer in his head. He communicates this answer to the horse with very subtle facial expressions that the horse can perceive. In this way it can "stamp" the answers on the ground.

If, however, one's thinking is even more accurate than that of contemporary mathematical sciences, one might ask this lecturer how he could *prove* his theory. It would be impossible for him to do so. My own observations, on the other hand, led me to a different conclusion. I noticed that in his grey-brown coat Herr von Osten had large, bulging pockets out of which he took sugar lumps and small sweets that he shoved into the horse's mouth during his demonstrations. This ensured an especially close and intimate relationship, a physically-based affinity between steed and master. And due to this intimate physical relationship, this deep-seated attachment, which was constantly being renewed, a very close soul communication between a man and a horse came about. It was a far more intimate process than the horse's supposedly more intellectual and outward observation of its master's facial expressions. Indeed, a real communication from soul to soul had taken place.

If it is possible to observe such a phenomenon even in an animal, then you can comprehend the kind of soul communication that can exist in a little child, especially if permeated by deeply religious devotion. You must realize how everything the child makes its own grows from this religious mood, which is still fully centered within the physical body. Anyone who can observe how the child, with its inner attitude of religious surrender, surrenders to the influences of the surrounding world, and anyone who can discern in all these processes what the child individually pours into the static and dynamic forces, will discover precisely in this physical response the inherent impulses of its later destiny. However strange it may sound, what Goethe's friend Knebel in his old age once said to Goethe is still true:[1]

Anyone who looks back over one's past life will find that, when we have experienced a significant event and then look back at what led up to it, it becomes apparent that we were steered toward it. We find that it was not just one

1. Karl Ludwig von Knebel (1744–1834) German poet and tutor at the Court of Weimar.

previous step, but a whole series of previous steps, that now make it appear as if we had been striving toward the decisive event from a deep inner soul impulse.

If such an event is connected with someone else, the person concerned will think (provided one can extricate oneself from the turmoil of life and perceive the finer nuances of physical existence): This is not an illusion, or something I have dreamed up; but if, at a decisive moment in life, I have found another human being with whom I am more intimately connected than with other people, then I really have been seeking this person, whom I must have already known long before we met for the first time.

The most intimate matters in life are closely connected with how the child finds its way into the static and dynamic realm. If one can develop a faculty for observing such things, one will find that an individual's destiny already begins to be revealed in a strangely sense-perceptible form by how a child begins to place the feet on the ground, in how a child begins to bend the knees, or in the way a child begins to use the fingers. All of this is not merely outwardly or materially significant, but it reflects what is most spiritual in the human being.

When a child begins to speak, it adapts itself to a wider circle. In learning the mother tongue, this circle embraces all who share the same language. Now the child is no longer restricted to the narrow circle of people who provide a more intimate social background. In living into the mother tongue, the child also adapts to something broader than the static and dynamic forces. One could say that, in learning to speak, the child lives into its folk soul, into the genius of its mother tongue. And since language is thoroughly spiritual, the child still lives in something spiritual, but no longer in a spirituality only connected with the individual human being, something that is a matter of individual destiny, but something that receives the child into the wider circle of life.

When the child learns to think—well, with thinking we do not remain in the realm of the individual at all. In New Zealand, for example, people think exactly the same as we do here today. It is the entire Earth realm that we adapt ourselves to when as children we develop thinking from speech. In speaking we still remain within a smaller circle of life. In thinking, we enter the realm of humanity as a whole. This is how the child's life circles are expanded through walking, speaking, and thinking. And through discrimination one will find the fundamental links between the way a child adapts itself to the of static and dynamic forces, and its future destiny during earthly life.

Here we see the work of what we have been calling in anthroposophy the *I-being* of the human individual. For us, this term does not imply anything abstract, it merely serves to pinpoint a specifically human feature. Similarly, through the medium of language, we see something emerge in the human being that is entirely different from the individual I. Therefore we say that in language the human astral body is working. This astral body can also be observed in the animal world, but there it does not work in an outward direction. In the animal it is connected more with the inner being, creating the animal's form. We also create our form, but we take away a small part of this formative element and use it to develop language. In speech the astral body is actively engaged. And in thinking, which has this universal quality and is also specifically different from the other two faculties, something is happening where we could say that the human etheric body is working. Only when we come to human sense perception do we find the entire physical body in collaboration.

I do not mind if, for the time being, you treat these statements more or less as definitions. At this point it is not an

important issue, for we are not interested in splitting philosophical hairs. We are merely trying to indicate what life itself
reveals. And this needs to be based on a knowledge of the
human being that can lead us to a true form of education, one
that encompasses both theory and practice.

When looking at such a progression of development, we find
that the human being's highest member, the I, is the first to
emerge, followed by the astral body and etheric body. Furthermore, we can see how the soul and spiritual organization,
working in the I, astral, and etheric bodies, is working on the
physical body until the change of teeth. All three members are
working in the physical body.

The second dentition announces a great change that affects
the child's whole life. We can first observe it in a particular phenomenon. What would you say is the most striking factor of
early childhood? It is, as I have described it just now, the child's
physical-religious devotion to its environment. This is really
the most decisive characteristic. Then the child loses the baby
teeth, which is followed by years of developing a certain soul-
spiritual constitution, particularly in the years between the
change of teeth and puberty.

You see, what has been working physically during the first
period of life will later, after the child has gone through
puberty, reappear transformed as thought. The young child
cannot in any way yet develop the kind of thinking that leads
to an experience of religious devotion. During this time of
childhood—first before the change of teeth, but also continuing until puberty—these two things keep each other at a distance, so to speak. The child's thinking, even between the
change of teeth and puberty, does not yet take hold of the religious element. One could compare this situation with certain
alpine rivers that have their sources high up in the mountains
and that, on their way down, suddenly seem to disappear as

they flow through underground caves, only to reappear lower down along their further courses. What appears as a natural religious reverence during the years leading to the change of teeth withdraws inward, takes on an entirely transformed soul quality, and seems to disappear altogether. Only later in life, when the human being gains the capacity to consciously experience a religious mood, does it reappear, taking hold of a person's thinking and ideation.

If one can observe such transformations, one will find external observation even more meaningful. As I mentioned already in the first lecture, I am not at all against the more external forms of observation, which are fully justified. Yet, at the same time, we must realize that these methods cannot offer a foundation for the art of education. Experimental child psychology, for example, has discovered the curious phenomenon that children whose parents anxiously try to engender a religious attitude, who try to drum religion into their children, such children achieve poor results in their religion lessons at school. In other words, it has been established that the *correlation coefficient* between the children's accomplishments in religious instruction and the religious attitude of their parents is very low during the years spent in primary education.

Yet one look at human nature is enough to discover reasons for this phenomenon. No matter how often such parents may talk about their own religious attitude, no matter what beautiful words they may speak, it has no meaning for the child at all. They simply pass the child by. For anything directed to the child's reason, even if formulated in terms intended to appeal to the child's feelings, will fail to have any impact, at least until the time of the change of teeth. The only way of avoiding such heedlessness is for the adults around the child, through their actions and general behavior, to give the child the possibility to imitate and absorb a genuine religious element right into the finest articulation of the vascular system. This is then worked on inwardly, approximately between the seventh and fourteenth year. Like the alpine river flowing underground, it will surface again at puberty in the form of a capacity for conceptualization.

So we should not be surprised if a generous helping of outer piety and religious sentiment aimed at the child's well-being will simply miss the mark. Only the actions performed in the child's vicinity will speak. To express it somewhat paradoxically, the child will ignore words, moral admonitions, and even the parents' attitudes, just as the human eye will ignore something that is colorless. Until the change of teeth, the child is an imitator through and through.

Then, with the change of teeth, the great change occurs. What was formerly a physically based surrender to a religious mood ceases to exist. And so we should not be surprised when the child, who has been totally unaware of any innate religious attitude, becomes a different being between the change of teeth and puberty. But what I have pointed out just now can reveal that, only at puberty, the child reaches an intellectual mode of comprehension. Earlier, its thinking cannot yet comprehend intellectual concepts, because the child's thinking, between the change of teeth and puberty, can only unite with what is pictorial. Pictures work on the senses. Altogether, during the first period of life ending with the change of teeth, pictures of all the activities being performed within its environment work on the child. Then, with the onset of the second set of teeth, the child begins to take in the actual content presented in pictorial form. And we must pour this pictorial element into everything that we approach the child with, into everything we bring to the child through language.

I have characterized what comes toward the child through the element of statics and dynamics. But through the medium of language a much wider, an immensely varied element,

Don't talk about reverence, be in at

Don't be surprised by change in persona at ?

comes within reach of the child. After all, language is only a link in a long chain of soul experiences. Every experience belonging to the realm of language has an artistic nature. Language itself is an artistic element, and we have to consider this artistic element above everything else in the time between the change of teeth and puberty.

Don't imagine for a moment that with these words I am advocating a purely esthetic approach to education, or that I want to exchange fundamental elements of learning with all kinds of artificial or esthetically contrived methods, even if these may appear artistically justified. Far from it! I have no intention of replacing the generally uncultured element, so prevalent in our present civilization, with a markedly Bohemian attitude toward life. (For the sake of our Czech friends present, I should like to stress that I do not in any way associate a national or geographical trait with the term *Bohemian*. I use it only in its generally accepted sense, denoting the happy-go-lucky attitude of people who shun responsibilities, who disregard accepted rules of conduct, and who do not take life seriously.) The aim is not to replace the pedantic attitude that has crept into our civilization with a disregard of fundamental rules or with a lack of earnestness.

Something entirely different is required when one is faced with children between the change of teeth and puberty. Here one has to consider that at this age their thinking is not yet logical, but has a completely pictorial character. True to nature, such children reject a logical approach. They want to live in pictures. Highly intelligent adults make little impression on children aged seven, nine, eleven, or even thirteen. At that age, they feel indifferent toward intellectual accomplishment. On the other hand, adults with an inner freshness (which does not, however, exclude a sense of discretion), people of a friendly and kindly disposition do make a deep impression on children. People whose voices have a ring of tenderness, as if their words were caressing the child, expressing approval and praise, reach the child's soul. This personal impact is what matters, because with the change of teeth the child no longer surrenders solely to surrounding activities. Now a new openness awakens to what people are actually saying, to what adults say with the natural authority they have developed. This reveals the most characteristic element inherent in the child between the change of teeth and puberty.

Certainly you would not expect me, who more than thirty years ago wrote the book *Intuitive Thinking: A Philosophy of Freedom,* to stand here and plead authoritarian principles. Nevertheless, insofar as children between the change of teeth and puberty are concerned, authority is absolutely necessary. It is a natural law in the life of the souls of children. Children at this particular stage in life who have not learned to look up with a natural sense of surrender to the authority of the adults who brought them up, the adults who educated them, cannot grow into a free human beings. Freedom is won only through a voluntary surrender to authority during childhood.

Just as during the first period of life children imitate all of the surrounding activities, so also during the second period of life they follow the spoken word. Of course, this has to be understood in a general way. Immensely powerful spiritual substance flows into children through language, which, according to their nature, must remain characteristically pictorial. If one observes how, before the change of teeth, through first learning to speak, children dreamily follow everything that will become fundamental for later life, and how they wake up only after the change of teeth, then one can gain a picture of what meets children through the way we use language in their presence during the second period of life.

Therefore we must take special care in how, right at this stage, we work on children through the medium of language.

Everything we bring must speak to them, and if this does not happen, they will not understand. If, for example, you factually describe a plant to a young child, it is like expecting the eye to understand the word *red*. The eye can understand only the *color* red, not the word. A child cannot understand an ordinary description of a plant. But as soon as you tell the child what the plant is saying and doing, there will be immediate understanding. The child also has to be treated with an understanding of human nature. We will hear more about this later when we discuss the practical aspects of teaching. Here I am more concerned with presenting a basic outline.

And so we see how an image-like element pervades and unites what we meet in the child's threefold activity of walking, speaking, and thinking. Likewise, activities occurring around the child, which were at first perceived in a dreamy way, are also transformed, strangely enough, into pictures during this second period between the change of teeth and puberty. The child begins to dream, as it were, about the surrounding activities, whereas during the first period of life these outer activities were followed very soberly and directly, and simply imitated. And the thoughts of the child are not yet abstract, nor yet logical; they are also still pictures. Between the second dentition and puberty, children live in what comes through language, with its artistic and pictorial element. Thus, only what is immersed in imagery will reach the child. This is why the development of a child's memory is particularly strong at this age.

And now, once again, I have to say something that will make learned psychologists shudder inwardly and give them metaphorical goose flesh. That is, children receive their memory only with the change of teeth. The cause for such goose flesh is simply that these things are not observed properly. Someone might say, "What appears as memory in a child after the change of teeth surely must have already existed before, even more strongly, because the child then had an inborn memory, and all kinds of things could be remembered even better than later on." This would be about as correct as saying that a dog, after all, is really a wolf, and that there is no difference between the two. And if one pointed out that a dog has experienced entirely different living conditions and that, although descended from the wolf, it is no longer a wolf, the reply might be, "Well, a dog is only a domesticated version of a wolf, for the wolf's bite is worse than the dog's bite." This kind of thing would be somewhat analogous to saying that the memory of a child is stronger prior to the change of teeth than afterward. One must be able to observe actual reality.

What is this special kind of memory in the young child that later memory is descended from? It is still an inner habit. When taking in the spoken word, a refined inner habit is formed in the child, who absorbs everything through imitation. And out of this earlier, specially developed habit—which still has a more physical quality—a soul habit is formed when the child begins the change of teeth. It is this habit, formed in the soul realm, that is called memory. One must differentiate between habit that has entered the soul life and habit in the physical realm, just as one has to distinguish between dog and wolf—otherwise one cannot comprehend what is actually happening.

You can also feel the link between the pictorial element that the child's soul had been living within, as well as the newly emerging *ensouled habit*, the actual memory, which works mainly through images as well.

Everything depends, in all these matters, on keen observation of human nature. It will open one's eyes to the incisive turning point during the change of teeth. One can see this change especially clearly by observing pathological conditions in children. Anyone who has an eye for these things knows that children's diseases look very different from adult diseases. As a

rule, even the same outer symptoms in an ill child have a different origin than those in an adult, where they may appear similar, but are not necessarily the same. In children the
characteristic forms of illness all stem from the head, from
which they affect the remaining organism. They are caused by
a kind of overstimulation of the nerve-sense system. This is
true even in cases of children who have measles or scarlet fever.

If one can observe clearly, it will be found that when walking, speaking, and thinking exert their separate influences,
these activities also work from the head downward. At the
change of teeth, the head has been the most perfectly molded
and shaped inwardly. After this, it spreads inner forces to the
remaining organism. This is why children's diseases radiate
downward from the head. Because of the way these illnesses
manifest, one will come to see that they are a reaction to conditions of irritation or overstimulation, particularly in the nerve-
sense system. Only by realizing this will one find the correct
pathology in children's illnesses. If you look at the adult you
will see that illnesses radiate mainly from the abdominal-motor
system—that is, from the opposite pole of the human being.

Between the age when the child is likely to suffer from an
overstimulation of the nerve-sense system and in the years following sexual maturity—that is, between the change of teeth
and puberty—are the years of compulsory schooling. And
amid all of this, a kinship lives between the child's soul life and
the pictorial realm, as I have described it to you. Outwardly,
this is represented by the rhythmic system with its interweaving of breathing and blood circulation. The way that breathing
and blood circulation become inwardly harmonized, the way
that the child breathes at school, and the way that the breathing gradually adapts to the blood circulation, all of this generally happens between the ninth and tenth year. At first, until
the ninth year, the child's breathing is in the head, until,

through an inner struggle within its organism, a kind of harmony between the heartbeat and the breathing is established. This is followed by a time when the blood circulation predominates, and this general change occurs in the physical realm and in the realm of the child's soul.

After the change of teeth is complete, all of the forces working through the child are striving toward inwardly mobile imagery, and we will support this picture-forming element if we use a pictorial approach in whatever we bring to the child. And then, between the ninth and tenth years, something truly remarkable begins to occur; the child feels a greater relationship to the musical element. The child wants to be held by music and rhythms much more than before. We may observe how the child, before the ninth and tenth years, responds to music—how the musical element lives in the child as a shaping force, and how, as a matter of course, the musical forces are active in the inner sculpting of the physical body. Indeed, if we notice how the child's affinity to music is easily expressed in eagerly performed dance-like movements—then we are bound to recognize that the child's real ability to grasp music begins to evolve between the ninth and tenth years. It becomes clearly noticeable at this time. Naturally, these things do not fall into strictly separate categories, and if one can comprehend them completely, one will also cultivate a musical approach before the ninth year, but this will be done in the appropriate way. One will tend in the direction suggested just now. Otherwise the child aged nine to ten would get too great a shock if suddenly exposed to the full force of the musical element, if the child were gripped by musical experiences without the appropriate preparation.

We can see from this that the child responds to particular outer manifestations and phenomena with definite inner demands, through developing certain inner needs. In recognizing these needs, knowledge does not remain theoretical, but

becomes pedagogical instinct. One begins to see how here one
particular process is in a state of germination and there another
is budding within the child. Observing children becomes
instinctive, whereas other methods lead to theories that can be
applied only externally and that remain alien to the child.
There is no need to give the child sweets to foster intimacy.
This has to be accomplished through the proper approach to
the child's soul conditions. But the most important element is
the inner bond between teacher and pupil during the classroom time. It is the crux of the matter.

Now it also needs to be said that any teacher who can see
what wants to overflow from within the child with deep inner
necessity will become increasingly modest, because such a
teacher will realize how difficult it is to reach the child's being
with the meager means available. Nevertheless, we shall see that
there are good reasons for continuing our efforts as long as we
proceed properly, especially since all education is primarily a
matter of self-education. We should not be disheartened
because the child at each developmental stage reacts specifically
to what the external world—that is we, the teachers—wishes to
bring, even if this may assume the form of a certain inner opposition. Naturally, since consciousness has not awakened sufficiently at that age, the child is unaware of any inner resistance.
In keeping with their own nature, children, having gone
through the change of teeth, demand lesson content that has
form and coloring that satisfies what is overflowing from their
organisms. I will speak more about this later.

But one thing that children do not want—certainly not during the change of teeth—something they will reject with strong
inner opposition—is to have to draw on a piece of paper, or on
the chalkboard, a peculiar sign that looks like this: *A,* only to
be told that this is supposed to sound the same as what would
spontaneously come from one's own mouth [Ah!] when seeing

something especially wonderful! [2] For such a sign has nothing
whatever to do with the inner experience of a child. When a
child sees a combination of colors, feelings are immediately
stimulated. But if one puts something in front of a child that
looks like FATHER, expecting an association with what is
known and loved as the child's own father, then the inner being
of the child can feel only opposition.

How have our written symbols come about? Think about the
ancient Egyptians with their hieroglyphs that still retained some
similarity to what they were intended to convey. Ancient cunei-
form writing also still had some resemblance to what the signs
signified, although these were more expressive of the will-nature
of the ancient people who used them, whereas the Egyptian
hieroglyphs expressed more of a feeling approach. The forms of
these ancient writings, especially when meant to be read,
brought to mind the likeness of what they represented from the
external world. But what would children make of such weird
and ornate signs on the chalkboard? What could they have to do
with their own fathers? And yet the young pupils are expected to
learn and work with these apparently meaningless symbols. No
wonder that something in the child becomes resentful.

When children are losing their baby teeth, they feel least
connected with the kind of writing and reading prevalent in
our present stage of civilization, because it represents the results
of stylization and convention. Children, who have only
recently come into the world, are suddenly expected to absorb
the final results of all of the transformations that writing and
reading have gone through. Even though nothing of the many
stages of cultural progress that have evolved throughout the
ages has yet touched the children, they are suddenly expected
to deal with signs that have lost any connection between our

---

2. In German, the letter *A* is pronounced "ah" as in "father" or "star." — TRANS.

modern age and ancient Egypt. Is it any wonder, then, if children feel out of touch?

On the other hand, if you introduce children to the world of number in an appropriate way for their age, you will find that they can enter the new subject very well. They will also be ready to appreciate simple geometric forms. In the first lecture I have already noted how the child's soul prepares to deal with patterns and forms. Numbers can also be introduced now, since with the change of teeth a hardening of the inner system is occurring. Through this hardening, forces are being released and expressed outwardly in how the child works with numbers, drawing, and so on. But reading and writing are activities that are, initially, very alien to children at around the seventh year. Please do not conclude from what I have said that children should not be taught to read and write. Of course they must learn this because, after all, we do not educate the young for our benefit, but for life. The point is, how should this be done without countering human nature? We shall go into this question more thoroughly during the next few days. But, generally speaking, it is good if educators realize how alien many things are to a child's soul, things that we take from contemporary life and teach because we feel it is necessary for the children to know them.

This must not lead us into the opposite error of wanting to create an esthetic form of education, however, or declaring that all learning should be child's play. This is one of the worst slogans, because such an attitude would turn children into the kind of people who only play at life. Only dilettantes in the field of education would allow themselves to be taken in by such a phrase. The point is not to select certain tidbits out of play activities that are pleasing to an adult, but to connect with what is actually happening when a child is playing.

And here I must ask you a pertinent question. Is play mere fun or is it a serious matter for children? To a healthy child, playing is in no way just a pleasurable pastime, but a completely serious activity. Play flows earnestly from a child's entire organism. If your way of teaching can capture the child's seriousness in play, you will not merely teach in a playful way—in the ordinary sense—but you will nurture the earnestness of a child's play. What matters at all times is the accurate observation of life. Therefore it can be rather regrettable if well-meaning people try to introduce their pet ideas into the one branch of life that demands the closest observation of all—that is, education. Our intellectual culture has landed us in a situation where most adults no longer have any understanding of childhood, because a child's soul is entirely different from that of a thoroughly intellectualized adult. We must begin by finding the key to childhood again. This means that we must permeate ourselves with the knowledge that, during the first period of life until the change of teeth, the entire behavior of a child reveals a physically anchored religious quality; and after this, between the change of teeth and puberty, a child's soul life is attuned to all that has a pictorial quality, and it undergoes many artistic and esthetic changes during this period of life.

When a child has reached puberty, the astral body, which has been working through language until this point, now becomes free to work independently. Previously, the forces that work through the medium of language were needed to build up the inner organization of the child's body. But after puberty, these forces (which work also in many other spheres—in everything that gives form, in relation to both plastic and musical forms) become liberated, and are used for the activity of thinking. Only then does the child become an intellectualizing and logically thinking person.

It is clear that what flashes, streams, and surges through language in this way, delivers a final jolt to the physical body before becoming liberated. Look at a boy who is at this age and listen to how his voice changes during puberty. This change is just as decisive as the change of teeth in the seventh year. When the larynx begins to speak with a different vocal undertone, it is the astral body's last thrust—that is, the forces flashing and working through speech—in the physical body. A corresponding change also occurs in the female organism, but in a different way, not in the larynx. It is brought about through other organs. Having gone through these changes, the human being has become sexually mature.

And now the young person enters that period of life when what previously radiated into the body from the nerve-sense system is no longer the determining factor. Now it is the motor system, the will system—so intimately connected with the metabolic system—that takes the leading role. The metabolism lives in physical movements. Pathology in adults can show us how, at this later age, illnesses radiate mainly from the metabolic system. (Even migraine is a metabolic illness.) We can see how in adults illnesses no longer spread from the head, as they do in children. It does not matter so much where an illness manifests, what matters is to know from where it radiates into the body.

But during grade school (from about six to fourteen) the rhythmic system is the most actively engaged. During this time, everything living within the nerve-sense system on the one hand, and within the metabolic-limb system on the other, is balanced by the rhythmic system. This balancing activity of the rhythmic system encompasses what works through our physical movement, where processes of combustion continually occur, and are also balanced by the metabolism. This balancing activity also works in the metabolism's digestion of what will eventually enter the bloodstream and take the form of circulation. This all comes together in the breathing process, which has a rhythmical nature, in order to work back again finally into the nerve-sense process. These are the two polarities in human nature. The nerve-sense system on the one hand, the metabolic-limb system on the other, with the rhythmic system in between.

We have to consider this rhythmic system above all when dealing with children between the change of teeth and puberty. It is fully expressed during these years, and it is the healthiest of the human systems; it would have to be subjected to gross external interference to become ill.

In this respect, modern methods of observation again take the wrong course. Think of the recent scientific tests that study fatigue in children by means of fatigue coefficients. Let me repeat again at this point, to avoid misunderstandings, that I have no intention of running down modern methods of scientific investigation as such, nor of heaping scorn on its methods. In these experiments various degrees of fatigue are measured, for example, in gym or arithmetic classes, and so on. There is nothing wrong in discovering such factors, but they must not form the basis of one's teaching. One cannot arrange a time-table according to these coefficients because the real task of a teacher is very different. At this stage of childhood, the aim should be to work with the one system in the human being that never tires throughout a person's whole life. The only system prone to fatigue is the metabolic and limb system. This system does tire, and it passes its fatigue to the other systems. But I ask you, is it possible for the rhythmic system to tire? No, it must never tire, because if the heart were not tirelessly beating throughout life, without suffering fatigue, and if breathing were not continuous without becoming exhausted, we simply could not live. The rhythmic system does not tire.

If we tire our pupils too much through one or another activity, it shows that, during the age under consideration—between seven and fourteen years—we have not appealed strongly enough to the rhythmic system. This middle system again lives entirely in the pictorial realm and is an outer expression of it. If you fail to present arithmetic or writing lessons imaginatively, you will tire your pupils. But if, out of an inner freshness and at a moment's notice, you can call up powers of imagery in the children, you will not tire them. If they nevertheless begin to droop, the source of their fatigue is in their motor system. For example, the chair that a child sits on might be pressing too hard, or the pen may not fit the hand properly. There is no need to calculate through pedagogical psychology how long a child can engage in arithmetic without undue strain. The important thing is that the teacher knows how to teach the various subjects in harmony with the pupils rhythmic system, and how, through knowledge of the human being, the lesson content can be presented in the appropriate form.

This can become possible only when we recognize that the pupil awakens to the intellectual side of life only with the advent of sexual maturity, and that between the change of teeth and puberty the teachers have to guide through personal example as they bring to their pupils what they wish to unfold within them. Consequently, a pedagogy that springs from a true knowledge of the human being has to be largely a matter of the teachers' own inner attitudes—a pedagogy destined to work on the teachers' own moral attitudes. A more drastic expression of this would be: The children in themselves are all right, but the adults are not! What is needed above all has already been put into words at the end of the first lecture. Instead of talking about how we should treat children, we should strive toward a knowledge of how we, as teachers and educators, ought to conduct ourselves. In our work we need forces *of the heart*. Yet it is not good enough to simply declare that, instead of addressing ourselves to the intellect of our pupils we now must appeal to their hearts, in both principle and method. What we really need—and this I wish to emphasize once more—is that we ourselves have our hearts in our pedagogy.

Lecture Four

In our previous meetings I have tried to direct you into what we understand as knowledge of the human being. Some of what is still missing will surely find its way into our further considerations during this conference. I have also told you that this knowledge of the human being is not the kind that will lead to theories, but one that can become human instinct, ensouled and spiritual instinct that, when translated into actions, can lead to living educational principles and practice. Of course, you must realize that in giving lectures of this kind, it is only possible to point the way, in the form of indications, to what such knowledge of the human being can do for the furtherance of practical teaching. But just because our primary goal is toward practical application, I can give only broad outlines, something that is very unpopular these days. Few people are sufficiently aware that anything expressed in words can, at best, be only a hint, a mere indication of what is far more complex and multifarious in actual life.

If we remember that young children are essentially ensouled sense organs, entirely given over in a bodily-religious way to what comes toward them from the surrounding world, we shall see to it that, until the change of teeth, everything within their vicinity is suitable to be received through their senses, thereafter to be worked on inwardly. Most of all, we have to be aware that whenever the child perceives with the senses, at the same time the child also absorbs the inherent moral element of what is perceived through the soul and spirit. This means that at the approach of the change of teeth, we have already set the scene for the most important impulses of later life, and that when the child enters school, we are no longer faced with a blank page but with one already full of content.

And now that we are moving more toward the practical aspects of education, we have to consider that between the change of teeth and puberty nothing entirely original can be initiated in the child. Instead, it is the teacher's task to recognize the impulses already implanted during the first seven years. They have to direct these impulses toward what is likely to be demanded of the pupils in their later lives. This is why it is of such importance for teachers to be able to perceive what is stirring within their pupils; for there is more here than meets the eye in these life-stirrings when children enter school. Teachers must not simply decide what they are going to do, or which method is right or wrong. It is far more important for them to recognize what is inwardly stirring and moving in these children—in order to guide and develop them further.

Naturally, this is bound to raise a question, which we have thus far been unable to answer in the Waldorf school since it has not yet become practical to open a kindergarten. The work entailed in bringing up and educating children from birth until the change of teeth is certainly most important. But since in the Waldorf school we are already facing great difficulties in coping with the demands involved in teaching children of official school age, we cannot possibly think of opening a kindergarten, because every year we also have to open a new class for our oldest pupils.[1] So far we have started with an eight-year course in the Waldorf school. At present we could not possibly entertain the idea of also opening a kindergarten, or something similar, as a preparatory step for our first grade. People who take a somewhat lighthearted view of these things may be of the opinion that the only thing needed is to begin with a nursery or kindergarten, and the rest will surely follow. But things are not that simple. A fully comprehensive, yet detailed program is needed that covers both the pedagogical and practical aspects of teaching in a nursery class. To devote oneself to such a task is impossible as long as a new class has to be added every year.

The seriousness and responsibility involved in the so-called movements for school reform is recognized by far too few people. To unprofessional, although well-meaning persons, it seems enough to voice demands, which are easy enough to make. In our day, when everybody is so clever—I am not being sarcastic, I am quite serious—nothing is easier than to formulate demands. All that is needed in our society, which is simply bursting with cleverness, is for eleven or twelve people—even three or four would be brainy enough—to come together to work out a perfect program for school reform, listing their requirements in order of priority. I have no doubt that such theoretical demands would be highly impressive. These programs, compiled in the abstract today in many places, are very cleverly conceived. Because people have become so intellectual, they excel in achievements of an external and abstract kind.

But if one judges these matters out of real life experience and not intellectually, the situation is not unlike one where a number of people have come together to discuss and decide what

---

1. The first kindergarten in the Waldorf School was opened a short time later under Steiner's direction.

the performance of an efficient stove should be. Obviously they would come up with a whole list of "categorical imperatives," such as that the stove must be capable of heating the room adequately, it must not emit smoke, and so on. But, though the various points made may be convincing enough, knowledge of them alone would hardly result in the necessary know-how to light it, keep it going, and control its heat. To be able to do this one has to learn other things as well. In any case, depending on the location of the room, the condition of the chimney and possibly on other factors as well, it may not even be possible to fulfill the conditions so competently set forth.

But this is how most of the programs for school reform are arrived at today—more or less in an equally abstract manner as the requirements for the hypothetical stove. This is the reason why one cannot contravene them, for they no doubt contain much that is correct. But to cope with the practical needs of an existing school is something very different from making demands that, ideally speaking, are justified. Here one does not have to deal with how things ought to be, but with a number of actual pupils. Here one has to deal—allow me to mention it, for it is all part of school life—with a definite number of teachers of varying gifts and abilities. All this has to be reckoned with. There is no problem in planning a program for school reform in the abstract. But the concrete reality is that only a certain number of gifted teachers are available and it may not even be possible for *them* to fulfill the demands agreed upon in theory.

This fundamental difference between life as it is and an intellectual approach to it is something our present society is no longer able to appreciate. Because it has become so accustomed to an intellectual interpretation of life, it can no longer perceive this quality, least of all where it is most patently present. Anyone who is aware of the great difference between theory and practice will detect the worst excesses of impractical theories in our present business life. In reality the structure of today's business life has become as theoretical as can be. Those in control grasp power with robust hands. They use their elbows and often brutally push through their theoretical policies. This goes on until the business is ruined. In the economic sphere it is possible to proceed intellectually. But in a situation where one meets life in the raw, such as in a school (where it is not simply a case of helping oneself, but where existing impulses have to be worked on) even the most beautiful theories are of little use unless they offer the possibility of working pragmatically and out of a truly individual knowledge of what the human being is. This is the reason why teachers whose heads are full of pedagogical theories are usually least fit for practical classroom situations. More capable by far are those who still teach out of a certain instinct, teachers who, out of their natural love for children, are able to recognize and to meet them. But today it is no longer possible to rely on instinct, unless it is backed by spiritual knowledge. Modern life has become too complex for such a way of life, which would be possible only under more primitive conditions, under conditions almost bordering on the level of animal life.

All this has to be considered if one wishes to see what is being presented here in the right light, as a really practical form of pedagogy. Generally speaking, education has followed in the footsteps of our modern civilization, which has gradually become more and more materialistic. A symptom of this is the frequent use of mechanical methods in preference to organic methods, and this just during the early years of childhood up to the change of teeth, which is the most impressionable and important time of life. We must not lose sight of the fact that up to the second dentition the child lives by imitation. The serious side of life, with all its demands in daily work, is re-enacted in deep earnestness by the child in its play, as I mentioned yesterday. The difference between a child's play and an adult's work is that an adult's contribution to society is governed by a sense of purpose and has to fit into outer demands, whereas the child wants to be active simply out of an inborn and natural impulse. Play activity streams outward from within. Adult work takes the opposite direction, namely inwards from the periphery. The significant and most important task for grade school consists in just this gradual progression from play to work. And if one is able to answer in practical terms the great question of how a child's play can gradually be transformed into work, one has solved the fundamental problem during those middle years from seven to fourteen.

In their play, children mirror what happens around them; they want to imitate. But because the key to childhood has been lost through inadequate knowledge of the human being, all kinds of artificial play activities for children of kindergarten age have been intellectually contrived by adults. Since children want to imitate the work of the adults, special games have been invented for their benefit, such as "Lay the Little Sticks," or whatever else these things are called. These artificial activities actually deflect the child's inner forces from flowing out of the organism as a living stream that finds a natural outlet in the child's desire to imitate those who are older. Through all kinds of mechanical manipulations children are encouraged to do things not at all suitable to their age. Particularly during the nineteenth century, programs for preschool education were determined that entailed activities a child should not really do; for the entire life of a preschool class revolves around the children adapting to the few people in charge, who should behave naturally so that the children feel stimulated to imitate whatever their teachers do.

It is unnecessary for preschool staff to go from one child to another and show each one what to do. Children do not yet want to follow given instructions. All they want is to copy what the adult does, so the task of a kindergarten teacher is to adjust the work taken from daily life so that it becomes suitable for the children's play activities. There is no need to devise occupations like those adults meet in life—except under special circumstances—such as work that requires specialized skills. For example, children of preschool age are told to make parallel cuts in strips of paper and then to push multi-colored paper strips through the slits so that a woven colored pattern finally emerges. This kind of mechanical process in a kindergarten actually prevents children from engaging in normal or congenial activities. It would be better to give them some very simple sewing or embroidery to do. Whatever a young child is told to do should not be artificially contrived by adults who are comfortable in our intellectual culture, but should arise from the tasks of ordinary life. The whole point of a preschool is to give young children the opportunity to imitate life in a simple and wholesome way.

This adjustment to adult life is an immensely important pedagogical task until kindergarten age, with all its purposefulness, so that what is done there will satisfy the child's natural and inborn need for activity. To contrive little stick games or design paper weaving cards is simple enough. It is a tremendously important and necessary task to whittle down our complicated forms of life, such as a child does when, for example, a little boy plays with a spade or some other tool, or when a girl plays with a doll; in this way children transform adult occupations into child's play, including the more complicated activities of the adult world. It is time-consuming work for which hardly any previous "spade-work" has thus far been done. One needs to recognize that in children's imitation, in all their sense-directed activities, moral and spiritual forces are working—artistic impulses that allow the child to respond in an entirely individual way.

to clean up after her or not clean up after her.

Give a child a handkerchief or a piece of cloth, knot it so that a head appears above and two legs below, and you have made a doll or a kind of clown. With a few ink stains you can give it eyes, nose, and mouth, or even better, allow the child to do it, and with such a doll, you will see a healthy child have great joy. Now the child can add many other features belonging to a doll, through imagination and imitation within the soul. It is far better if you make a doll out of a linen rag than if you give the child one of those perfect dolls, possibly with highly colored cheeks and smartly dressed, a doll that even closes its eyes when put down horizontally, and so on. What are you doing if you give the child such a doll? You are preventing the unfolding of the child's own soul activity. Every time a completely finished object catches its eye, the child has to suppress an innate desire for soul activity, the unfolding of a wonderfully delicate, awakening fantasy. You thus separate children from life, because you hold them back from their own inner activity. So much for the child until the change of teeth.

When children enter school, we are very likely to meet a certain inner opposition, mainly toward reading and writing, as mentioned yesterday. Try to see the situation through a child's eyes. There stands a man. He has black or blond hair. He has a forehead, nose, eyes. He has legs. He walks, and he holds something in his hands. He says something. He has his own thought-life. This is father. And now the child is supposed to accept that this sign, FATHER represents an actual father. There is not the slightest reason why a child should do so.

Children bring formative forces with them, forces eager to flow out of the organism. Previously, these forces were instrumental in effecting the wonderful formation of the brain with its attendant nervous system. They accomplished the wonderful formation of the second teeth. One should become modest and ask how one could possibly create, out of one's own resources, these second teeth on the basis of the first baby teeth; what sublime powers of wisdom, of which we are totally unaware, work in all these forces! The child was entirely surrendered to this unconscious wisdom weaving through the formative forces. Children live in space and time, and now, suddenly, they are supposed to make sense of everything that is imposed on them by learning to read and write.

It is not proper to lead children directly into the final stages of our advanced culture. We must lead them in harmony with what wants to flow from their own being. The right way of introducing the child to reading and writing is to allow the formative forces—which up to its seventh year have been working upon the physical organization and which now are being released for outer soul activities—to become actively engaged.

For example, instead of presenting the child directly with letters or even complete words, you draw something looking like this:

In this way, by appealing to the formative forces in its soul, you will find that now the child can remember something that has actual meaning, something already grasped by the child's formative forces. Such a child will tell you, "That is a mouth." And now you can ask it to say, "Mmmouth." Then you ask it to leave out the end part of the word, gradually getting the child to pronounce "Mmm." Next you can say, "Let us paint what you have just said." We have left something out, therefore this is what we paint:

And now let us make it even simpler:

It has become the letter *M*.
Or we might draw something looking like this.

The child will say, "Fish." The teacher responds, "Let's make this fish simpler." Again one will ask the child to sound only the first letter, in this way obtaining the letter *F*. And so, from these pictures, we lead to abstract letter forms.

There is no need to go back into history to show how contemporary writing evolved from ancient pictography. For our pedagogical purposes it is really unnecessary to delve into the history of civilization. All we have to do is find our way—helped along by wings of fantasy—into this method, and then, no matter what language we speak, choose some characteristic words that we then transform into pictures and finally derive the actual letters from them. In this way we work together with what the child wants inwardly during and immediately after the change of teeth. From this you will understand that, after having introduced writing by drawing a painting and by painting a drawing (it is good for children to use color immediately because they live in color, as everyone who deals with them knows), one can then progress to reading. This is because the entire human being is active in writing. The hand is needed, and the whole body has to adapt itself—even if only to a slight degree; the entire person is involved. Writing, when evolved through painting-drawing, is still more concrete than reading. When reading—well, one just sits, one has already become like a timid mouse, because only the head has to work. Reading has already become abstract. It should be evolved by degrees as part of the whole process.

But if one adopts this method in order to work harmoniously with human nature, it can become extraordinarily difficult to withstand modern prejudices. Naturally, pupils will learn to read a little later than expected today, and if they have to change schools they appear less capable than the other students in their new class. Yet, is it really justified that we cater to the views of a materialistic culture with its demands concerning what an eight-year-old child should know? The real point is that it may not be beneficial at all for such a child to learn to read too early. By doing so, something is being blocked for life. If children learn to read too early, they are led prematurely into abstractions. If reading were taught a little later, countless potential sclerotics could lead happier lives. Such hardening of the entire human organism—to give it a simpler name—manifests in the most diverse forms of sclerosis later in life, and can be traced back to a faulty method of introducing reading to a child. Of course, such symptoms can result from many other causes as well, but the point is that the effects of soul and spirit on a person's physical constitution are enhanced hygienically if the teaching at school is attuned to human nature. If you know how to form your lessons properly, you will be able to give your students the best foundation for health. And you can be sure that, if the methods of modern educational systems were healthier, far fewer men would be walking around with bald heads!

People with a materialistic outlook give too little attention to the mutual interaction between the soul-spiritual nature and the physical body. Again and again I want to point out that the tragedy of the current materialistic attitude is that it no longer understands the material processes—which it observes only externally—and that it no longer recognizes how a moral element enters the physical. Already the way the human being is treated—one could almost say *mistreated*—by our natural science is likely to lead to misconceptions about what a human being is. You need only think of the usual kinds of illustrations found in contemporary textbooks on physiology or anatomy, where you see pictures of the skeleton, the nervous system, and the blood circulation. The way these are drawn is very suggestive, implying that they are a true representation of reality. And yet, they do not convey the actual facts at all—or at best, only ten percent of them, because ninety percent of the human body consists of liquid substances that constantly flow and, consequently, cannot be drawn in fixed outlines. Now you may say, "Physiologists know that!" True, but this knowledge remains within the circle of physiologists. It does not enter society as a whole, particularly because of the strongly suggestive influence of these illustrations.

People are even less aware of something else. Not only does solid matter make up the smallest portion of our physical body, while the largest part by far is liquid, but we are also creatures of air every moment of our lives. One moment the air around us is inside us, and in the next, the air within our body is outside again. We are part of the surrounding air that is constantly fluctuating within us. And what about the conditions of warmth? In reality we have to discriminate between our solid, liquid, gaseous, and warmth organizations. These distinctions could be extended further, but for now we will stop here.

It will become evident that meaningless and erroneous ideas are maintained about these matters when we consider the following: If these illustrations of the skeleton, the nervous system, and so on, really represented the true situation—always implying that the human being is a solid organism—if this were really the whole truth, then it would be little wonder if the moral element, the life of the soul, could not penetrate this solid bone matter or this apparently rigid blood circulation. The physical and moral life would require separate existences. But if you include the liquid, gaseous, and warmth organizations in your picture of the individual, then you have a fine agent, a refined entity—for example, in the varying states of warmth—that allows the existing moral constitution to extend also into the physical processes of warmth. If your picture is based on reality, you will come to find this unity between what has physical nature and what has moral nature. This is what you have to remember when working with the growing human being. It is essential to have this awareness.

And so it is very important for us to look at the totality of the human being and find our way, unimpeded by generally accepted physiological-psychological attitudes. It will enable us to know how to treat the child who will otherwise develop inner opposition toward what must be learned. It should be our aim to allow our young students to grow gradually and naturally into their subjects, because then they will also love what they have to learn. But this will happen only if their inner forces become involved fully in these new activities.

The most damaging effects, just during the age of seven to nine, are caused by one-sided illusions, by fixed ideas about how certain things should be taught. For example, the nineteenth century—but this was already prepared for in the eighteenth century—was tremendously proud of the new phonetic method of teaching reading that superseded the old method of making words by adding single letters—a method that was again replaced by the whole-word method. And because today people are too embarrassed to openly respect old ways, one will hardly find anyone prepared to defend the old spelling method. According to present opinion, such a person would be considered an old crank, because enthusiasm about an old-fashioned spelling method is simply not appropriate. The phonetic and the whole-word method carry the day. One feels very proud of the phonetic method, teaching the child to develop a feeling for the quality of sounds. No longer do young pupils learn to identify separate letters, such as *P, N,* or *R*; they are taught to pronounce the letters as they sound in a word.

There is nothing wrong with that. The whole-word method is also good, and it sometimes even begins by analyzing a complete sentence, from which the teacher progresses to separate words and then to single sounds. It is bad, however, when these things become fads. The ideas that underlie all three methods are good—there is no denying that each has its merits. But what is it that makes this so? Imagine that you know a person only from a photograph showing a front view. The picture will have created a certain image within you of that person. Now imagine that another picture falls into your hands, and someone tells you that this is the same person. The second picture shows a side view and creates such a different impression that you may be convinced that it could not be the same person. Yet in reality both photographs show the same individual, but from different angles. And this is how it always is in life: everything has to be considered from different angles. It is easy to fall in love with one's own particular perspective because it appears to be so convincing. And so one might, with good reasons, defend the spelling method, the phonetic method, or the whole-word method to the extent that anyone else with an opposite opinion could not refute one's arguments. Yet even the best of reasons may prove to be only one-sided. In real life, everything has to be considered from the most varied angles.

If the letter forms have been gained through painting drawings and drawing paintings, and if one has gone on to a kind of phonetic or whole-word method—which is now appropriate because it leads the child to an appreciation of a wholeness, and prevents it from becoming too fixed in details—if all this has been done, there is still something else that has been overlooked in our materialistic climate. It is this: the single sound, by itself, the separate *M* or *P,* this also represents a reality. And it is important to see that, when a sound is part of a word, it has already entered the external world, already passed into the material and physical world. What we have in our soul are the sounds as such, and these depend largely on our soul nature. When we pronounce letters, such as the letter *M,* for example, we actually say *"em."* Ancient Greeks did not do this; they pronounced it *"mu."* In other words, they pronounced the auxiliary vowel *after* the consonant, whereas we put it *before* the consonant. In Middle Europe today, we make the sound of a letter by proceeding from the vowel to the consonant, but in ancient Greece only the reverse path was taken.[2] This indicates the underlying soul condition of the people concerned.

Here we have a significant and important phenomenon. If you look at language, not just from an external or utilitarian perspective (since language today has become primarily a way of transmitting thoughts or messages, and words are hardly more than symbols of outer things), and if you return to the soul element living in the word—living in language as a

---

2. In several European languages the vowel sound added to a consonantal letter is pronounced either before or after the consonant (that is, *em,* but *dee*). It is conceivable that here the stenographer may have omitted the word "often," and the text may have read "In Middle Europe today we *often* make the sound of a letter by proceeding from the vowel to the consonant...." — TRANS.

whole—you will find the way back to the true nature of the so-called sound; every sound with a quality of the consonant has an entirely different character from a vowel sound.

As you know, there are many different theories explaining the origin of language. (This is a situation similar to photographs taken from different angles.) Among others, there is the so-called *bow-wow theory*, which represents the view that words imitate sounds that come from different beings or objects. According to this theory, when people first began to speak, they imitated characteristic external sounds. For example, they heard a dog barking, "bow-wow." If they wanted to express a similar soul mood they produced a similar sound. No one can refute such an idea. On the contrary, there are many valid reasons to support the bow-wow theory. As long as one argues only from this particular premise, it is indisputable. But life does not consist of proofs and refutations; life is full of living movement, transformation, living metamorphosis. What is correct in one particular situation can be wrong in another, and vice versa. Life has to be comprehended in all its mobility.

As you may know, there is another theory, called the *ding-dong theory*, whose adherents strongly oppose the bow-wow theory. According to this second theory, the origin of language is explained in the following way: When a bell is struck, the ensuing sound is caused by the specific constitution of its metal. A similar mutual relationship between object and sound is also ascribed to human speech. The ding-dong theory represents more of a feeling into the materiality of things, rather than an imitation of external sounds.

Again, this theory is really correct in certain respects. Much could be said for either of these theories. In reality, however, language did not arise exclusively according to the ding-dong theory nor the bow-wow theory, although both theories have elements of truth. Many other related factors would also have to be considered, but each theory, in isolation, gives only a one-sided perspective. There are many instances in our language that exemplify the ding-dong theory, and many others where sound represents an imitation, as in "bow-wow," or in the "moo" of lowing cattle. The fact is, both theories are correct, and many others as well. What is important is to get hold of life as it actually is; and if one does this, one will find that the bow-wow theory is more related to vowels, and the ding-dong theory related more to consonants. Again, not entirely, however; such a statement would also be one-sided, because eventually one will see that the consonants are formed as a kind of reflection of events or shapes in our environment, as I have indicated already in the little book *The Spiritual Guidance of the Individual and Humanity.*[3] Thus the letter *F* is formed as a likeness of the fish, *M* as a likeness of the mouth, or *L* like leaping, and so on.

To a certain extent, the origin of the consonants could be explained by the ding-dong theory, except that it would have to be worked out in finer detail. The vowels, on the other hand, are a way of expressing and revealing a person's inner nature. The forms of the letters that express vowel sounds do not imitate external things at all, but express human feelings of sympathy and antipathy. Feelings of joy or curiosity are expressed, therefore, by the sound *EE*; amazement or wonder; "I am astonished!" is expressed by *AH*; *A* [as in *path*] expresses "I want to get rid of something that irritates me." *U* [as in *you*] expresses "I am frightened." *I* [as in *kind*] conveys "I like you."

Vowels reveal directly feelings of sympathy and antipathy. Far from being the result of imitation, they enable human beings to communicate likes and dislikes. When hearing a

---

3. Rudolf Steiner, *The Spiritual Guidance of the Individual and Humanity,* Anthroposophic Press, Hudson, NY, 1992.

dog's threatening bark, human beings—if their feelings are like those of the dog—adapt their own experiences to the *bow-wow* sound of the dog, and so on. Vocalizing leads outward from within, whereas forming consonants represents a movement inward from outside. Consonants reproduce outer things. Simply by making these sounds, one is copying outer nature. You can confirm this for yourselves if you go into further detail.

Since all of this applies only to sounds rather than words, however, you can appreciate that, when using the analytic method, one is actually going from the whole word to the original soul condition. In general, we must always try to recognize what the child at each stage is requesting inwardly; then we can proceed in freedom—just as a good photographer does when asking clients to look in many different directions in order to capture their personalities while taking their pictures (and thereby making these sessions so tedious!). Similarly, a complete view is essential if one wants to comprehend the human being in depth.

With the whole-word method one gains only the physical aspect. With the phonetic method one approaches the soul realm. And—no matter how absurd this may sound—with the spelling method one actually enters the realm of the soul. Today this last method is, of course, seen as a form of idiocy; without a doubt, however, it is more closely related to the soul than the other methods. It must not be applied directly, but needs to be introduced with a certain pedagogical skill and artistry that avoids an overly one-sided exercise in conventional pronunciation of the letters. Instead, the child will gain some experience of how letters came about, and this is something that can live within the formative forces, something real for the child. This is the core of the matter. And if young pupils have been taught in this way they will be able to read in due time—perhaps a few months after the ninth year. It doesn't really matter if they cannot read earlier, because they have learned it naturally and in a wholesome way. Depending on the various children's responses, this stage may occur a little earlier or later.

The ninth year marks the beginning of a smaller life cycle— the larger ones have already been spoken of several times. They are: from birth to the change of teeth; from the change of teeth to puberty; and from then into the twenties. These days, how-ever, by the time young people have reached their twenties, one no longer dares speak to them of another developmental phase, which will peak after the age of twenty-one. This would be considered a pure insult! At that age they feel fully mature—they already publish their own articles in newspapers and magazines. And so one has to exercise great discretion in speaking about life's later stages of development. But it is important for the educator to know about the larger life peri-ods and also about the smaller ones contained in them. Between the ninth and the tenth years, but closer to the ninth, one of the smaller periods begins, when a child gradually awakens to the difference between self and the surrounding world. Only then does a child become aware of being a sepa-rate I. All teaching before this stage should therefore make the child feel at one with the surroundings.

The most peculiar ideas have been expressed to explain this phenomenon. For example, you may have heard people say, "When a young child gets hurt by running into a corner, the reaction is to hit the corner." An intellectual interpretation of this phenomenon would be that one hits back only if one has consciously received a hurt or an injury consciously inflicted. And this is how the child's response in hitting a table or other object is explained. This kind of definition always tempts one to quote the Greek example of a definition of the human being—that is, a human being is a living creature who has two legs but no feathers. As far as definitions go, this is actually correct. It leads us back into the times of ancient Greece. I won't go into details to show that present definitions in physics are often not much better, because there children are also taught frequently that a human being is a creature that walks on two legs and has no feathers. A boy who was a bit brighter than the rest thought about this definition. He caught a cockerel, plucked its feathers, and took it to school. He presented the plucked bird, saying, "This is a human being! It is a creature that walks on two legs and has no feathers." Well, definitions may have their uses, but they are almost always one-sided.

The important thing is to find one's way into life as it really is—something I have to repeat time and again. The point is that before the ninth year a child does not yet distinguish between self and surroundings. Therefore one cannot say that a little child, when hitting the table that caused it pain, imagines the table to be a living thing. It would never occur to a child to think so. This so-called animism, the bestowal of a soul on an inanimate object—an idea that has already crept into our history of civilization—is something that simply does not exist. The fantastic theories of some of our erudite scholars, who believe they have discovered that human beings endow inanimate objects with a soul, are truly astonishing. Whole mythologies have been explained away in light of this theory. It strikes one that people who spread such ideas have never met a primitive person. For example, it would never occur to a simple peasant who has remained untouched by our sophisticated ways of life to endow natural phenomena with a soul quality. Concepts such as *ensouling* or *animation of dead objects* simply do not exist for the child. The child feels alive, and consequently everything around the child must also be alive. But even such a primitive idea does not enter children's dim and dreamy consciousness. This is why, when teaching pupils under nine, you must not let the children's environment and all that it contains appear as something separate from them. You must allow plants to come to life—indeed, everything must live and speak to children, because they do not yet distinguish between themselves and the world as a whole.

It is obvious from this that, before the ninth year, you cannot reach children with any kind of intellectual descriptions. Everything has to be transformed into pictures, into fresh and living pictures. As soon as you go on to a more direct description, you will not achieve anything during the eighth to ninth year. This approach becomes possible only later. One has to find the way into each specific life period. Until the ninth year children only understand a pictorial presentation. Anything else bypasses them, just as sound bypasses the eye. But between the ninth and tenth years, as children gradually become more aware of their own identity, you can begin to present more factual descriptions of plants. However, it is not yet possible to describe anything that belongs to the mineral kingdom, because the children's newly evolving capacity to differentiate between self and world is not yet strong enough to allow them to comprehend the significant difference between what is inherently alive and what belongs to the dead mineral world. Children at this stage can only appreciate the difference between themselves and a plant. Thereafter you can gradually progress to a description of animals. But again this has to be done so that the introduction to the animal world remains real for the child.

Today there is an established form of botany, and along with that a tendency to introduce this subject just as it is in the lower grades. This is done out of a kind of laziness, but it really is an appalling thing to present the botany of adults to younger classes. What is this botany of ours in actuality? It is made up of a systematic classification of plants, arranged according to certain accepted principles. First come the *fungi*, then *algae*, *ranunculaceae*, and so on—one family placed neatly next to another. But if such a branch of science (which itself may be quite acceptable) is taught to young children in schools, it is almost like arranging different kinds of hairs, plucked from a human body, and classifying them systematically according to where they grew—behind the ears, on the head, on the legs, and so on. Following this method, you might manage to build up a very impressive system, but it would not help you understand the true nature of hair. And because it seems almost too obvious, one might easily neglect to relate the various types of hair to the human being as an entity. The plant world does not have its own separate existence either, because it is part of Earth. You may think that you know the *laburnum* from what you find about it in a botany book. I have no objections to its botanical classification. But to understand why its blossoms are yellow, you have to see it on a sunny slope, and you have to include in your observation the various layers of soil from which it grows. Only then can you realize that its yellow color is connected with the colors of the soil from which it grows! But in this situation you look at this plant as you would look at hair growing out of a human body. Earth and plants—as far as the child knows them already—remain one. You must not teach adult botany in the lower grades, and this means you cannot describe a plant without, at the same time, also talking about the Sun shining on it, about climatic conditions and the configuration of the soil—in a manner appropriate to the age of the child, of course.

To teach botany as this is done in demonstrations—taking isolated plants, one next to another, violates the child's nature. Even in demonstrations everything depends on the choice of object to be studied. The child has an instinctive feeling for what is living and for what is truly real. If you bring something dead, you wound what is alive in the child, you attack a child's sense of truth and reality. But these days there is little awareness of the subtle differences in these qualities. Imagine contemporary philosophers pondering the concept of being, of existence. It would make very little difference to them whether they chose a crystal or a blossom as an object of contemplation, because both of them *are*. One can place them both on a table, and both things *exist*. But this is not the truth at all! In regard to their being, they are not homogeneous. You can pick up the rock crystal again after three years; it *is* by the power of its own existence. But the blossom is not as it appears at all. A blossom, taken by itself, is a falsehood in nature. In order to assign existence or being to the blossom, one has to describe the entire plant. By itself, the blossom is an abstraction in the world of matter. This is not true of the rock crystal. But people today have lost the sense for such differentiations within the reality of things.

Children, however, still have this feeling by instinct. If you bring something to children that is not a whole, they experience a strange feeling, which can follow them into later life. Otherwise Tagore would not have described the sinister impression that the amputated leg had on him in his childhood. A human leg in itself does not represent reality, it has nothing to do with reality. For a leg is only a leg as long as it is part of a whole organism. If cut off, it ceases to be a leg.

Such things have to become flesh and blood again so that, by progressing from the whole to the parts, we comprehend reality. It can happen all too easily that we treat a separate part in a completely wrong way if we isolate it. In the case of botany in the lower grades, therefore, we must start with the Earth as a whole and look at the plants as if they were the hair growing out of it.

With regard to the animal world, children cannot relate properly to the animal at all if you follow the common method of classification. Since animal study is introduced only in the tenth or eleventh year, you can then expect a little more from the children. But to teach the study of animals according to the usual classification has little real meaning for students of that age, even if this method is scientifically justified. The reality is that the entire animal kingdom represents a human being that is spread out. Take a lion, for example; there you see a one-sided development of the chest organization. Take the elephant; here the entire organization is oriented toward a lengthening of the upper lip. In the case of the giraffe, the entire organization strives toward a longer neck. If you can thus see a one-sided development of a human organic system in each animal, and survey the entire animal kingdom all the way down to the insect (one could go even further, down to the "geological" animals, though *Terebratulida* are not really geological animals any more) then you will realize that the entire animal kingdom is a "human being," spread out like an opened fan, and the human physical organization makes up the entire animal kingdom, folded together like a closed fan. This is how one can bring the mutual relationship between the human being and the animal into proper perspective. Putting all this into such few words is making it into an abstraction, of course. You will have to transform it into living substance until you can describe each animal-form in terms of a one-sided development of a specific human organic system. If you can find the necessary strength to give your pupils a lively description of animals in this sense, you will soon see how they respond. For this is what they want to hear.

And so the plants are linked to the Earth as if they were the hair of the Earth. The animal is linked to the human being and seen as a one-sided development of various human organic systems. It is as if human arms or legs—and in other instances, the human nose or trunk, and so on—had grown into separate existences in order to live as animals on Earth. This is how pupils can understand the animal-forms. It will enable the teacher to form lessons that are attuned to what lives in the growing human being, in the children themselves.

A question is asked concerning religious instruction.

RUDOLF STEINER: A misunderstanding has arisen from my preliminary remarks about child development and religious impulses. So far nothing has been said in my lectures about religious instruction itself, because I began to talk only today about the practical application of the Waldorf way of teaching. I told you that there is a kind of *physical-religious* relationship (I called it *bodily-religious*) between children and their environment. Furthermore, I said that what young children exercised—simply because of their organism—entered the sphere of thinking only after puberty, after approximately the fourteenth or fifteenth year. What manifests at first in a physical-spiritual way, continues in a hidden existence, and re-emerges in the thinking realm in approximately the fifteenth year; I compared that with an underground stream surfacing again on lower ground. For an adult, religion is closely linked to the thinking sphere. If teaching, however, is to be in line with the child's natural development, what will emerge later must already be carefully prepared for during an earlier stage. And thus the question arises: Bearing these laws of human development in mind, how should the religion lessons be planned for the students between the ages of six and fourteen? This is one of the questions that will be addressed in coming lectures.

In anticipation, however, I would like to say that we must be clear that the religious element is simply inborn in the child, that it is part of the child's being. This is revealed particularly clearly through the child's religious orientation until the change of teeth, as I have already described it. What has eventually become religion in our general civilization—taken in an adult sense—belongs naturally to the world of ideas, or at least depends on ideation for its substance, which, true enough, lives primarily in the adult's feeling realm. Only after the fourteenth year is the adolescent mature enough to appreciate the ideal quality and substance of religion. For the class teacher (grades one through eight) the important question thus arises: How should we arrange our religion lessons? Or, more precisely: What part of the child must we appeal to through religion lessons during the time between the seventh and fourteenth years?

During the first life period, until the change of teeth, we directly affect the child's physical organization through an educational influence. After puberty, fundamentally speaking, we work on the powers of judgment and on the adolescent's mental imagery. During the intervening years we work upon the child's feeling life. This is why we should lead the child into this period with a pictorial approach, because pictures work directly in soul life (*Gemüt*).[4] The powers of mental imagery mature only gradually, and they have to be prepared well before their proper time. What we now have to do in religion lessons is appeal, above all, to the children's soul life, as I will describe it in regard to other subjects tomorrow. The question is: How do we do it?

We work on the children's *soul life* by allowing them to experience feelings of sympathy and antipathy. This means that we act properly by developing the kind of sympathies and antipathies between the seventh and fourteenth years that will lead

---

4. *Gemüt* is virtually untranslatable. Rudolf Steiner said "this *Gemüt lives in the center of soul life.*" A dictionary defines it as "heart, soul, or mind." But these must be considered as one rather than as three separate things. Thus, one can read *Gemüt* as "soul," that is, heart and mind together.

finally to proper judgments in the religious sphere. And so we avoid *Thou shalt* or *Thou shalt not* attitudes in our religion lessons, because it has little value for teaching a child of this age. Instead we arrange lessons so that feelings of sympathy are induced for what the child is meant to do. We do not explain our real aims to children. Using the pictorial element as medium, we present children with what fills them with feelings of sympathy in a heightened sense, as well as in a religious sense. Likewise, we try to induce feelings of antipathy toward what they are not meant to do.

In this way, on the strength of feelings of right or wrong, and always through the pictorial element, we try to direct the young students gradually from the divine-spiritual in nature, through the divine-spiritual in the human being, toward having children make the divine-spiritual their own. This has to all reach the child through the life of soul, however, certainly until eighth grade. We must avoid a dogmatic approach and setting up moral commandments. We must do all we can to prepare the child's soul for what should develop later on as the adult faculty of forming sound judgments. In this way we will do far more for the child's future religious orientation than by presenting religious commandments or fixed articles of faith at an age when children are not yet ready for them. By clothing our subject in images, thus preparing the ground for what in later life will emerge as religious judgment, we prepare our students for the possibility of comprehending through their own spirituality what they are meant to grasp as their own innermost being—that is, their religious orientation. Through appealing to the children's soul-life in religion lessons—that is, by presenting our subject pictorially rather than through articles of faith or in the form of moral commandments—we grant them the freedom to find their own religious orientation later in life. It is extremely important for young people, from puberty right into their twenties, to have the opportunity to lift, by their own strength, what they first received through their soul life—given with a certain breadth from many perspectives—into conscious individual judgments. It will enable them to find their own way to the divine world.

It makes all the difference whether children, during the age of authority, are brought up in a particular religious belief, or whether, by witnessing the teacher's underlying religious attitude, they are enabled "to pull themselves up like a plant on its tendrils," and thus develop their own morality later in life. Having first found pleasure or displeasure in what was finally condensed into an attitude of *Thou shalt* or *Thou shalt not*, and having learned to recognize, through a pictorial contemplation of nature, how the human soul becomes free through an inner picture of a divine-spiritual weaving in nature and in history, a new stage is reached where young people's own images and ideas can be formed. In this way the possibility is given of receiving religious education out of the center of life itself. It is something that becomes possible only after puberty has been reached.

The point is that future stages have to be prepared for properly—that is, based on the correct insight into human nature. In my lectures I have used the comparison of the river that disappears underground and resurfaces at a lower level. During the first seven years the children have an inborn religious attitude. This now enters the depths of their souls, becoming part of them, and does not resurface in the form of thinking until the arrival of puberty. During the second life period we must work into the depths of the students' souls through what is revealed to our individual insights. In this way we prepare them to grow into religious adults. We impede this process if we do not offer our students the possibility to find their own religious orientation later on. In every human being there is an individual orientation toward religion, which, after the fifteenth year, has to be gradually won. Our task is to prepare the ground so that this can happen properly. That is why, at this age, we have to treat the religion lessons just as we do the lessons in the other subjects. They must all work on the child's soul through the power of imagery; the child's soul life has to be stimulated. It is possible to introduce a religious element into every subject, even into math lessons. Anyone who has some knowledge of Waldorf teaching will know that this statement is true. A Christian element pervades every subject, even mathematics. This fundamental religious current flows through all of education.

Because of prevailing circumstances, however, we have felt it necessary to come to the following arrangement regarding religious instruction. I would like to point out once more that Waldorf schools are not ideological but pedagogical schools, where the basic demand is that our teaching methods be in harmony with the child's nature. Thus we neither wish nor intend to teach our students to become anthroposophists. We have chosen anthroposophy to be the foundation simply because we believe that a true method of teaching can flow from it. Our Catholic students are taught by visiting Catholic priests, and our Protestant students by visiting Protestant ministers. Waldorf students, whose parents are free-thinkers, and who otherwise would not receive any religious instruction at all, are given religion lessons by our own teachers. The surprising fact has emerged, however, that nearly all of our Waldorf students now attend the religion lessons presented by Waldorf teachers. They have all flocked to the so-called "free" religion lessons, lessons that, in their own way, comprise what permeates all of our teaching.[5]

---

5. *Free*, as used here means "nonsectarian."

These free religion lessons have certainly caused us a great deal of concern. Our relationship to the school is very unusual regarding these lessons. We consider all the other subjects as necessary and intrinsic to our education from the point of view of the principles and methods resulting from anthroposophical research. But, regarding the free religion lessons, we feel that we are on the same footing as the visiting Catholic or Protestant teachers. In this sense, Waldorf teachers who give religion lessons are also "outsiders." We do not want to have an ideological or confessional school, not even in an anthroposophical sense. Nevertheless, anthroposophical methods have proven to be very fertile ground for just these free religion lessons, in which we do not teach anthroposophy, but in which we build up and form according to the methods already characterized.

Many objections have been raised against these free religion lessons, not least because so many children have changed over from the denominational to the free religion lessons. This has brought many other difficulties with it, for, despite our shortage of teachers, we had to find among our existing staff one new religion teacher after another. It is hardly our fault if pupils desert their denominational religion lessons because they wish to join the free religion lessons. The obvious reason is that the visiting religion teachers do not apply Waldorf methods, and the right methods are always the decisive factor, in religious instruction as well.

A further question is asked about religious lessons.

RUDOLF STEINER: The characteristic mark of Waldorf education should be that all educational questions and problems are considered only from the pedagogical angle, and religion lessons are no exception. The Reverend Mr. X would certainly acknowledge that the two directions mentioned, namely the possibility of replacing religion lessons by moral instruction on the one hand, and that of denominational schools on the other, have been raised from very different viewpoints. The suggestion of replacing religious instruction with lessons in moral conduct is usually presented by those who want to eliminate religion altogether, and who maintain the opinion that religion has become more or less superfluous. On the other hand, a tendency toward religious dogma can easily cause a longing for denominational schools. Neither of these are pedagogical points of view.

In order to link them a little more precisely to the aspect of teaching method, I would like to ask: What constitutes the pedagogical point of view? Surely it is the assumption that a human being is not yet complete during the stage of childhood or youth—something very obvious. A child has to grow gradually into a full human individual, which will be achieved only during the course of life. This implies that all potential and dormant faculties in the child should be educated—and here we have the pedagogical point of view in its most abstract form.

If someone who represents the purely pedagogical outlook that results from insight into human nature were to now declare that a child comes into the world with an inborn kinship to the religious element, and that during the first seven years the child's corporeality is steeped in religion, only to hear a call for replacing religion lessons by lessons in ethics, it must strike such a person as if those who hold such an idea would be unwilling to exercise a human limb, say a leg, because they had concluded that the human being needs to be trained in every respect except in the use of legs! To call for the exclusion of an essential part of the human being can only stem from a fanatical attitude, but never from a real pedagogy. Insofar as only pedagogical principles are being defended and pedagogical impulses scrutinized here, the necessity of religious teaching certainly follows from the pedagogical point of view. This is why we have established the free religion lessons for those children who, according to the regulations of the school authorities, would otherwise have been deprived of religious instruction, as already stated. Through this arrangement, and because all the children belonging to this category are attending the free religion lessons, there is no student in the Waldorf school who does not have religious instruction. This procedure has made it possible for us to bring back the religious life into the entire school.

To speak of the proper cultivation of the religious life at school, and to counter the effects of the so-called "religion-free enlightenment," by appealing to the inborn religious disposition in the young, may be the best way forward to a religious renewal. I consider it a certain success for the Waldorf school to have brought religion to the children of religious dissidents. The Catholic and Protestant children would have received religious instruction in any case, but it really was not at all easy to find the appropriate form that would enable us to open this subject to all our children. It was strived for only from the pedagogical point of view.

Lecture Five

Between the ages of seven and approximately fourteen, the teacher's main concern must be directed toward the students' evolving life of feeling. It is really very important that educators acquire the ability to create the kind of mental imagery that can guide pupils through the tender transitional stages characteristic of this period.

When children enter school, remnants of the previous "bodily-religious mood," as I call it, still exist. There is still a longing in children to absorb through the senses everything happening in their surroundings; this perceiving, which is transformed into imitation, then connects with listening for what comes from the natural authority of the teacher. Truth, at this stage, is not based on the child's judgment, but comes in the guise of what the naturally revered authority of the teacher says. Similarly, what is considered false simply agrees with what this freely accepted authority considers false. This also applies to what is seen as beautiful or ugly, good or evil. Children can only develop the faculty of independent judgment in adulthood if they have gone through the experience of looking up to the voice of authority with uncritical veneration. Of course I am not referring to any kind of enforced authority here; the authority I am speaking of must never be imposed externally. And if, in some cases, an authoritarian approach is necessary for the sake of general society, the child should not be aware of it. The child must always feel secure in looking up with total confidence to the teacher's authority or that of another adult in charge. Everything has to be supported by this tender relationship to authority from the day the child enters the first grade until the ninth year, and especially during the seventh to ninth years. This relationship should be preserved even longer, but between the ninth and tenth years it will necessarily change somewhat.

Within this same context we must now look at another point. During the initial period of life—that is, from birth until the change of teeth—the child lives like one great multifaceted sense organ, but as a sense organ where will forces were working in every moment of life. For me to use the expression "a sense organ where will forces are working," may sound strange, but this is only because of the complete inadequacy of what we are told by contemporary physiology and the popular ideas derived from it. Today one does not associate will forces with the function of the human eye, for example. Nevertheless, even in the eye, the perceived image is due to will activity. The same is true of the functioning of every other sense organ: will-substance is instrumental in creating the inner sense impressions. The task of a sense organ, first of all, is to expose itself, or the human being, passively to the external world's influences. But within every sense organ an inner activity also occurs that has a will nature.

This will element works very intensively throughout the child's whole body until the change of teeth. It also remains active after this event, with the result that, between entering school and the ninth year, this predominant will element in the child will tolerate only an approach to external nature and to the human being that is entirely human and pictorial. This is why we introduce not aesthetics but a thoroughly artistic element, especially in the younger classes. We do this by allowing children to use liquid colors from the very beginning, even if this practice is likely to cause rather uncomfortable consequences in the classroom. We let children handle colors because, by putting them on paper next to one another—not according to preconceived notions, but simply from an instinctive sense of color; and through the ensuing inner satisfaction, they work in harmony with their own formative forces. When given this opportunity, children reveal a wonderful instinct for painting artistic color combinations, and these soon show the teacher how to direct children's efforts toward drawing with colored pencils from which writing can eventually evolve.

But one thing children at this age cannot do is follow explanations; they have no understanding for this at all. If a teacher tries to explain the subjects during the first school years, the children will react by becoming blunted and dull. This approach simply does not work. On the other hand, everything will go smoothly if, rather than explaining the subject matter, one forms the content into a story, if words are painted with mental images, and if rhythm is brought into one's whole way of teaching. If the teachers' relationship to music is not restricted to music in a narrow sense, but if they can introduce a musical element into their teaching—if their lessons are permeated by beat, rhythm, and other less obvious musical qualities—then children will respond spontaneously and with acute understanding. On the other hand, if the teachers who introduce the world by appealing to feeling in their students were to speak now of the human being as a separate entity, the children would feel inwardly resentful. They would reject it; indeed, they could simply not bear it. What children really want during this stage is for everything they learn about—even if it is part of inorganic nature—to be presented in living, human terms.

The inner horror (I think one can put it that strongly) of facing a description of the human being remains with the child until about the twelfth year. From the ninth to the twelfth year we can use what I described yesterday as the content for the lessons. As long as we present it imaginatively we can speak about the plant world in terms of hair growing out of the Earth, and we can introduce animal study by showing how in every animal form we can see a part of the human organism, but specialized in a one-sided way. At this stage, however, we must not study the human being directly as an object, because children are not yet ready for this. Only toward the twelfth year do they experience a dim longing to gather together the entire animal kingdom in order to discover synthesis of the animal world in the human being. This can form the new content for the classes, then, following the eleventh and twelfth years.

For you to be told that teachers should relate parts of the human organization to certain animal forms before their pupils have reached the necessary maturity to study the human being as a separate entity may sound contradictory, but life is full of such apparent contradictions. It is correct, nevertheless, to proceed in this way until the great moment comes when teachers can show their students how what is concentrated within one single human individual, is spread out over all of the animal kingdom. To allow children to experience very intensely such decisive moments in life is tremendously important in teaching; and one of these moments is the realization, passing through the child's soul, that the human being as seen physically is both the extract and the synthesis of the entire animal world, but on a higher level. The inner experience of such a climb over a childhood peak—if I may use this comparison—is more important than acquiring knowledge step by step. It will have a beneficial effect for the rest of the child's life. But because of the way our times have developed in an external scientific direction, there is little inclination to look so intimately at human nature. Otherwise things would not happen as they do in our civilization, especially in modern spiritual life. You only need to consider what I emphasized in our first meeting.

Until the seventh year, soul forces are working in all of the child's physical processes, concluding to a certain extent during the change of teeth. I have compared this with a solution that forms a sediment at the bottom of a container. The precipitate represents the denser parts, while a more refined solution remains above it. The two substances have separated from each other. Similarly, until the change of teeth, we can look at the child's physical and etheric bodies as still forming a homogeneous solution until the physical is precipitated, leaving the etheric free to work independently.

But now too much soul substance might be retained by the physical body. Part of the soul substance must always remain behind, because the human physical body must be permeated by soul and spirit throughout life. But too much soul and spiritual substance could be retained so that too little of it remains in the upper region. The result is a human being whose physical body is oversaturated with soul substance and whose soul and spiritual counterpart has become too insubstantial. This condition is met far too frequently, and with the necessary insight one can see it clearly in children between seven and fourteen. But in order to see this, one must be able to distinguish exactly between the coarser and the more refined components of our human organization.

It is essential today that our society develops a physiology backed by a strong enough psychology and a psychology that is not abstract, but supported by the necessary background of physiology. In other words, one has to be able to recognize the interrelationship between body and soul; otherwise an amateurish physiology and an equally amateurish psychology will result. Because of this lack of ability to see clearly through the human being, contemporary scientific life has produced two such dilettante branches of science. The reciprocal effect between them has resulted in "dilettantism squared," or as it is also called, *psychoanalysis*.

Just as a number multiplied by itself is that same number squared, so also a dilettante physiology, when multiplied by dilettante psychology, equals psychoanalysis. This is the secret behind the origin of psychoanalysis. I am not saying this to cast aspersions on psychoanalysis. Things could hardly have been otherwise because, due to our present day scientific climate, society lives in a time when psychology has become too diluted and physiology too dense. Seen in this light, physiology, rather than becoming a genuine branch of science, assumes the role of the precipitate from what should have remained as a homogeneous solution. This is only a picture, but I hope that you understand it.

We cannot avoid the need to be clear about how the growing human being develops, and about how we have to give appropriate attention to each particular stage in the life of children. Thus, we find that between the ninth and twelfth years children are receptive to whatever comes to them as pictures. Until about the ninth year they want to participate in the formation of the picture—they will not yet play the role of spectators. During this time teachers have to work with their students in such a living way that their joint efforts, in and of themselves, already have a pictorial quality. It doesn't matter whether actual picture-making is involved, such as painting, drawing, or similar activities; all of the work, the lessons themselves, must form a picture. And then, between the ninth and tenth years, the children develop a new sense for a more external presentation of the pictorial element, and this is when we may appropriately introduce botany and animal study. Those two subjects in particular must be presented pictorially and imaginatively; and the more one can do this, the better one is as a teacher for children between nine and twelve—in contrast to what one finds in the usual textbooks on botany, where a great lack of imagery is displayed. Portraying the plant world in its many forms with true imagination is very rewarding, because to achieve this requires that one be "co-creative."

This sharing in the world's creativity is just the thing our present culture awaits. People in the middle of life come to me, again and again, full of despair because they cannot comprehend anything pictorially. This shortcoming can be traced back to childhood when their needs were not adequately met.

It is much too easy for the world to laugh when we say that the human being consists of a physical body, etheric body, astral body, and I-being. As long as one merely evaluates these matters with the yardstick of ordinary science, one cannot help but laugh. This is very understandable. But considering the serious tangle of our civilization, one would expect at least some willingness to look for what cannot be found elsewhere. There are many instances of apparent conundrums. Of course, it is easy enough to denigrate the following description of the human being: The physical body is born at birth. It develops through body-bound religiosity, by imitation, until the change of teeth. During these early years the etheric body and all the other forces are fully engaged in working on the child's physical body; they are soul and spiritual forces working in the child. The astral body is born only at puberty, and gains its independent existence from that time on. And as far as the human I is concerned—this is something that can be spoken of with certain reservations only—the I is fully born only after the twentieth year of life. Although it may be wisest to remain silent about this last point when talking to young people engaged in their first years of academic study, it is nevertheless an unalterable fact.

If one does not know the characteristic differences between the four members of the human being, one is likely to look at these differentiations as being nonsense—or at least, something highly superfluous. This changes, however, as soon as one knows about the whole human being. You see, if we look at physical matter we find that its main characteristic is its exertion of a certain pressure. I could equally say that it occupies space. It presses on other matter, pushing it. It also presses on our body, and we experience this pressure through the sense of touch. Physical matter exerts pressure.

The nature of the etheric has a quality all its own. During the last forty or fifty years natural science has seen the etheric as a rather peculiar phenomenon. If one were to speak about all the theories formulated concerning the essence of the etheric, one would be kept busy for a long time. This has already reached the degree that many people assert that the etheric is essentially the same as the principles of mathematics and mechanics that work in space, existing merely as some kind of linear force. To many investigating minds, the essence of the etheric is not much more than differential quotients flying around in space, or at least something that is mathematically calculable.

As you can see, much hard thinking has delved into the question of what the etheric is, and this in itself is admirable enough. However, as long as one continues along these lines, nothing of real significance will be discovered about the etheric. One has to know that the etheric has the characteristic of being the polar opposite of pressure; it has the effect of suction. It always has the tendency to expedite physical matter out of space, to annihilate it. This is the characteristic feature of the etheric. Physical matter fills up space, and the etheric gets rid of space-occupying matter. It could be called *negative matter*, but in a qualitative sense and not from a quantitative perspective.

This applies also to the human etheric body. Our relationship to the physical and etheric bodies consists of our constantly destroying and renewing ourselves. The etheric continually destroys material substance, and the physical body builds it up again. This statement contradicts the law of conservation of energy, which is generally accepted today. I am mentioning this only in passing, but it is a fact, nevertheless, that this law of conservation of energy is not compatible with the inner nature of the human being, and that it contradicts the truth. Strictly speaking, this law applies only to the inorganic realm. Within the organic world it is only true of the iron particles in the blood serum, but not concerning the whole human being, in whom a constant oscillation occurs between the suction process of the etheric, whose forces destroy matter, and the restoration affected by the physical body.

The astral body not only draws in space but—strange as it sounds—it draws in time! It has the quality of leading backward in time. This will be clearer to us if we consider an older person's life. Imagine that you were, let's say, fifty years old. In your astral body, forces are always at work, leading you back to earlier times in your life, taking you back to times before puberty. Fifty-year-olds do not experience their present age in their astral body, but actually experience themselves as eleven, twelve, thirteen, or fourteen again. These past ages radiate back to them through the backward-leading activity of their astral bodies. This is the secret of life. In reality we grow older only with regard to the physical body, and with the etheric body and its oscillations. The astral body, however, leads us back again and again to previous stages of life. Regarding the astral body we are all still "adult children." If we imagine the course of our lives expressed symbolically in the form of a tube, and if we have reached a certain point, say aged fifty, then our adult childhood shines right into our fifties, because the astral body always takes us back in time.

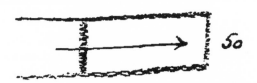

In the astral body, one always lives backward, but this retrospective life naturally begins only with the advent of puberty. If one can earnestly accept this in all earnestness, then one will appreciate its implications for education, and will give students something that will serve their later lives. Whatever one decides to do with them would then be seen in the context of their entire lives, even if they live to the age of ninety! This awareness will endow teachers with an appropriate sense of responsibility. It is this feeling of responsibility, arising from the knowledge of what one is really doing, that truly matters. However, this awareness can be developed only if teachers learn to recognize the hidden interconnections that affect human life. And if this happens, teachers will not assert that children should be taught only what they can comprehend fully. Such an attitude is truly appalling if one considers the true nature of the human being; pedagogical textbooks and handbooks written from the perspective of concrete demonstrations can lead one to despair. There the aim is always to come down to the level of the children's present stage of development and to treat everything so that they will see through them in every detail. This method deprives children of immensely important values for life, as anyone can see who recognizes how childhood is related to human life as a whole.

Let's take the example of a child who, at the age of eight, has accepted something that could not yet be comprehended, accepted something simply on the strength of a love and respect for the teacher, simply because whatever the teacher says must be right and good. Here, love for the teacher—or sympathy—was the vehicle for inner acceptance; the child may not understand the matter fully until sometime around the age of thirty-five. It is not easy to speak about such things to modern people, because they tend to disagree with the idea that sufficient maturity is gained only in the thirty-fifth year of life for understanding certain matters. It is nevertheless the truth, however, that only in the thirty-fifth year is one mature enough to understand certain things, things that one accepted as a child out of love for a teacher. Again, at this age one has experiences that result from the astral body's regressive forces. Something arises from within, a kind of a mirror reflection that, in reality, is a return to the days of childhood. It is like the arising of an inner vision. One is thirty-five years old, has become mature, and from the depths of one's soul there comes the realization: Only now do I understand what I accepted on trust when I was eight.

This ability to understand something that, permeated with love, has thus lived in one's being for many years, has a tremendously revitalizing effect on one's life. We can give this potential force of rejuvenation to children by safeguarding their inborn feeling for authority—so that such feeling can become a vehicle for love and sympathy—and also by giving children what they cannot yet fully comprehend, but will gradually ripen during the coming years of life. Such interconnections are not recognized by teachers who bring to their classes only what lies within their pupils' present capacity to understand. On the other hand, the opposite view is equally wrong and out of place. A teacher who knows human nature would never tell a child, "You cannot yet understand this." One must never resort to such a remark, because one can always clothe what one has to say in an appropriate garment if the necessary rapport has been established with the students.

If the pedagogy we are speaking of here becomes instinctive, one will know just what to say at the right moment. Above all, one will avoid sharply defined or rigid concepts. It is really appalling when a teacher's ideas and concepts have been worked out to the degree that they are no longer adaptable or flexible. They would have an effect similar to the effect of iron gloves forced onto a child's little hands, preventing them from growing naturally. We must not chain children's minds to finished concepts, but give them concepts that can grow and expand further. We must give them living concepts that can be transformed. But this can be achieved only through an imaginative approach in every subject, certainly until the twelfth year; then the method of teaching I have thus far sketched for you will encourage you to use language creatively, to draw helpful drawings on the blackboard or to take up a paintbrush to make colorful illustrations of what you want to communicate. But there must always be an awareness that everything a teacher brings has to be inwardly mobile and capable of remaining so; for one must recognize that, with the approach of the twelfth year (actually very close to the twelfth year), something new begins to develop, and that is the sense for cause and effect.

Before the approach of the twelfth year, the concept of causality does not exist in the minds of children. They have an eye for what is mobile. They can apprehend ideas that are flexible, and they can perceive what comes in the form of pictures or music; anything connected with causality, however, makes no sense to them until about the twelfth year. Consequently, this concept must be avoided at all costs until this time, and then we may consider a newly emerging understanding for the relationship between cause and effect. Only at that time do children begin to have their own thoughts about various things. Previously they saw the world in pictures; but now something begins to dawn that will light up only at puberty—that is, the life of thinking and the ability to form judgments, which is closely connected with thinking.

Between the change of teeth and puberty, children live primarily in the realm of feeling; before the change of teeth, they live in the region of the will, which, while still far removed from the sphere of thinking, is intimately connected with the fact that children imitate their surroundings. But what enters the child's being physically at that time also contains moral and spiritual forces, which became firmly established in the child's organism. This is why, during the tenth and eleventh years (and in most cases until the beginning of the twelfth year) it is impossible to communicate knowledge that demands an understanding of causality. Consequently, one should not introduce students to the mineral kingdom until around the twelfth year. Also, concepts connected with physics should not be explored before that age, although these have to be prepared for earlier through imagery that bypasses causality. Anything relating to cause and effect in the inorganic world can be grasped by children only around the twelfth year. This is one side of the problem.

We meet the other side when teaching history. Around the twelfth year it is impossible to awaken in students an understanding of the complex fabric of historical interconnections. Until that age it is wise for teachers to present graphic descriptions of historical personages whose actions, due to their goodness, truth, and other qualities of greatness, will stimulate sympathy or, in the case of negative qualities, antipathy in the souls of children. At this stage, historical content should appeal, above all, to the students' feelings. This can be accomplished by a wise selection of historical personalities and events; these should, in themselves, present a complete story, which should nevertheless remain flexible in the students' minds (in the sense mentioned). Causal links between earlier and later historical events can be taught meaningfully only at the dawn of the regressive forces of the astral body; these forces come increasingly into their own after the fourteenth year. At about the twelfth year, children enter this reverse stream, and this is the time when one can begin to appeal to a sense of causality in history as well.

When this is done earlier (and closely connected with the concept of cause and effect is the formation of judgments) one puts something into motion that can become very damaging in later life. At first there is only the child's etheric body. Toward the twelfth year, the astral body slowly begins its process of birth, which is completed at puberty. But the etheric body was already fully developed before that. If you ask students to make judgments (which always have a *yes* or *no* quality), or if you have them remember prefabricated concepts, these will enter the etheric body instead of the still unborn astral body. But what else does the astral body carry? As you may conclude from the facts of sexual maturity, the astral body also carries human love. Love is, of course, already active in children before puberty, but it has not yet reached an independent existence, has not yet been born fully. Thus, critical judgments, with their attendant yes-or-no qualities, are instilled in the child's etheric body instead of in the astral body. On the other hand, when made at the right time, the astral body's power of love and benevolence becomes an integral part in forming judgments or criticisms. If you make the mistake of forcing children to form critical judgments—of making them decide between *yes* and *no*—too early, then you fill their etheric bodies with immature judgments. But the ether body is not benevolent. It draws in whatever is in its way. Indeed, in this context, it is even malicious; it has a destructive effect. And this is what you do to children when you ask them to decide yes-or-no judgments prematurely, because a yes-or-no judgment is always behind the concept of causality.

On the other hand, a historical process that is complete in itself, or historical characters who are vividly described, can simply be looked at in the way one looks at pictures. As soon as one links later historical periods to earlier ones, however, one has to make judgments, one has to reject or accept, and this choice always contains an element of yes or no. The final outcome of such premature judgment in children under the age of fourteen is an inner resentment toward judgments that are generally accepted by society. If the power of judging is developed too early, the judgments of others are received with a latent destructive force rather than with benevolence. These things demonstrate the importance of doing the right thing at the right time.

Keeping this in mind, let us again compare the animal with the human being. When looking at the animal's outer appearance, its form indicates everything it does. We can also observe the animal's behavior. But in the case of the human being, we have to look for inner causes. Since children are only mature enough to look for causes in the twelfth year, this is the proper time to present the animal world as a "spread-out human being," or the human being as the synthesis of the entire animal kingdom. This is an instance where the teacher is asked to affect an experience in the child that satisfies an inner demand and readiness at this particular stage.

But now you have to acknowledge that this marks a powerful reversal in the child's nature between the change of teeth and puberty. In a certain sense, the child's soul now proceeds entirely from within outward. Recall that, until the twelfth year, children could not stand listening to a description of the human being, and now they are beginning to look at themselves as mirrors of the world—and they do this *conceptually*, in the form of ideas. This new readiness for a portrayal of the human being—that is, a portrayal of themselves—really does represent a complete about-face of children's nature between the second dentition and puberty.

During this same time—roughly between the ninth and tenth years—another very important transition occurs in the child's life. Individually, this change can vary; in some children it doesn't happen until after the tenth year. Each child, instinctively, unconsciously, faces a kind of riddle of life. This change of direction from within outward, this new awareness of being a self surrounded by an external world—whereas previously these two aspects were woven together—is something the child does not experience consciously, but through inner doubts and restlessness, which make themselves felt at that time. Physically, the breathing becomes properly integrated into the blood circulation, as the two processes begin to harmonize and balance each other. The relationship between the pulse and breathing is established. This is the physical aspect. The soul and spiritual counterpart is a new kind of dependence of the child on help from teachers or educators. This appeal for help is not necessarily expressed by direct questions, but in a characteristic form of behavior.

And now the teacher is called on to develop the skill necessary to correctly weigh this great, but unspoken, life question that lives in every student, although differently in each individual. What is this great life question? Up to this point, the child's natural sense of authority resulted from the image of the teacher as representative and mediator for the whole world. For the child, the stars moved because the teacher knew the stars' movement. Things were good or evil, beautiful or ugly, and true or false because this was the teacher's assessment. Everything that came from the world had to find the child through the teacher, and this represented the only healthy relationship between teacher and child.

Now however, between the ninth and the tenth years—sometimes a little later—a question arises within the child's soul, not as a concept or idea, but as a feeling. "From where does my teacher receive all this knowledge?" At this moment the teacher begins to become transparent to the student, if I may say it pictorially. The child wants to see the world as living behind the teacher, who must not fail now to confirm the student's heartfelt conviction that the teacher is properly attuned to the world, and embodies truth, beauty, and goodness. At this stage, the unconscious nature of children tests the teacher as never before. They want to discover whether the teacher is truly worthy of representing the entire world.

Again, all this has to remain unspoken. If a teacher were ever to mention or allude to it, through explanations or in other ways, this would appear only as a sign of weakness to the child, whose present state of consciousness has not yet developed a sense of causality; anything that requires proof only shows weakness and inner uncertainty. It is unnecessary to prove what is experienced powerfully in the soul.

This is also true concerning the history of our civilization. I do not want to go into details now, but merely give you a dynamic impression; until a particular time during the Middle Ages, people knew the meaning of the Last Supper. For them there was no need for proof. Then the situation suddenly changed. When seen in the proper light, this just shows that a real understanding of this event no longer existed. If someone is caught red-handed, no one would have to prove that such person is a thief. But if a thief escapes unseen, then proof must be found before that person can be properly called a thief. Proof is always demanded in cases of uncertainty, but not for what the facts of life tell us directly. This is why it is so ludicrous whenever people try to find the inner connection between formal logic and reality. This is somewhat like looking for the inner connection between a path leading to a mountain, and the mountain itself; the path is there to allow the wanderer to reach the mountain, and then the mountain itself begins. Logic is there only for the sake of reaching reality, and reality begins where logic ends.

Awareness of these things is of fundamental importance. One must not make the mistake of wanting to prove to students, when they are going through this important stage in life, that the world is being truthfully interpreted for them. When adjusting to this new situation in the classroom, one has to bring about in the pupils an unreasoned conviction that the teacher knows even more than they had previously imagined. The proper relationship between teacher and students can be established once again, perhaps while surprising the children with an amiable off-hand remark about something new and unexpected, which will make them sit up and listen; this can now happen if students feel that, until now, their teacher has not yet shown his or her true courage at all, and can truly reach unexpected heights. One has to save some things for just such moments, so that the teacher's image will continue to command respect. The solution to an important question of life lies within the students' feeling that their teacher can grow beyond even the boundaries of the personality. Here also are the comfort and strength one must give to children at this stage, so that one does not disappoint the hopeful expectations with which they come. Inwardly, such children were longing for reassurance from the one person for whom they had already developed sympathy and love. If this critical moment goes unnoticed, teachers will have to go through the bitter experience of losing their authority and hold over students around the ages of nine to ten. They may well feel tempted, therefore, to prove everything they do, and this dreadful mistake will only make matters worse.

When this view of education has become second nature, one will also find other helpful guidelines. But whatever is presented in class has to cohere; it has to fit together. I have already told you that we allow our young children paint quite freely and naturally, out of their own formative forces—at first not with colored pencils but with liquid colors. Through this, one soon realizes how much children live within the world of colors. After a while, the young student will come gradually to experience something distant—something that draws us away into far distances—as blue. It goes without saying that the teacher must have experienced this quality of blue as well. Yellow and red seem to move toward the beholder. Children can already experience this in a very concrete way during the seventh or eighth year, unless they have been plagued with fixed tasks in drawing or painting. Of course, if you force children to copy houses or trees representationally, this color experience will soon be lost. But if one guides children so they can feel: Wherever I move my hand, there the color follows—then the type of material used is of secondary importance. Or: The color really begins to live under my fingers—it wants to spread a little further. Whenever such feelings can be drawn out in children's souls, one enables them to discover something fundamental and significant—that is, *color perspective*. A child will feel that the reddening yellow comes towards us, and that mauve-blue takes us further away. This is how one can livingly prepare the ground for something that must be introduced at a later stage—*linear perspective*; it is very harmful to teach this subject before students have had an intensive experience of color perspective. To teach them *quantitative* perspective without their first having inwardly absorbed *qualitative* perspective—which is inherent in the experience of color—has the thoroughly harmful effect of making them superficial.

But there are even further implications. If you prevent children from having an intensive experience of color perspective, they will not develop the necessary incentive while learning to read (always remembering the reservation expressed yesterday, that it is unnecessary to push a child into reading at the earliest possible time). These color experiences will stimulate mobility in the child's mental imagery, suppleness in feelings, and flexibility in the will activities. The child's entire soul life will become more sensitive and pliable. It may well be that, if you use the method of painting-drawing and drawing-painting, the child will not learn to read as quickly. But when the right time comes, reading will not be anchored too loosely, which can happen, nor too tightly, as if each letter were making a kind of a scratch upon the tender soul-substance of the child.

The important thing is that whatever is comprehended through soul and spiritual faculties should find its proper realm within the human being. We should never ask: What is the point of teaching the child to paint, if it will never be used in later life? This represents an entirely superficial view of life because, in reality, a child has every need for just this activity; if one wants to understand the complexity of a child's needs, one just has to know something about the spiritual background of the human being. Just as the expression "You can't understand this" should never be used when talking to children, so also there should never be a skeptical attitude among adults concerning what a child needs or does not need. These needs should be recognized as flowing from the human constitution itself; and if they are, one will respond with the right instinct. One will not worry unduly, either, if a child forgets some of what has already been learned, because knowledge is transmuted into capacities, and these are truly important later in life. Such capacities will not develop if you overload a child with knowledge. It is essential to realize—and actually practice—that one should impress in the student's memory only what is demanded by social life, that there is no purpose in overburdening the student's memory.

This brings us to the question concerning the relationship between the individual and society, national or ethnic background, and humanity as a whole. When addressing this problem, we must try to avoid harming human nature when blending external demands with our educational practice.

A question is asked regarding music lessons given to a seventeen-year-old girl.

RUDOLF STEINER: The essential thing is what Mister Baumann has already presented to us.[1] With the beginning of puberty and during the following years, a certain musical judgment takes the place of a previous feeling for music and of a general musical experience. The faculty of forming musical judgments emerges. This becomes very noticeable through the phenomenon characterized by Mister Baumann—that is, a certain self-observation begins to manifest, a self-observation of the student's own singing and, with it, the possibility of using the voice more consciously, and so on. This has to be cultivated methodically.

At the same time, however, something else becomes noticeable—that is, from this stage on, natural musical memory

---

1. Paul Baumann (1887–1964) music teacher at the Waldorf School in Stuttgart, Germany.

begins to weaken a little, with the effect that students have to make more effort to remember music. This is something that has to be especially remembered during music lessons. Whereas, before puberty the children's relationship to music was spontaneous and natural, and because of this their musical memory was excellent, some of them now begin to encounter difficulties—not in taking in music, but in remembering it. This needs to be addressed. One must try to go over the same music several times, not by immediate repetition, but intermittently.

Another characteristic sign at this particular stage is that, whereas previously the instrumental and vocal parts of a piece were experienced as a unity, after the sixteenth to seventeenth years they are listened to with clear discrimination. (From a psychological point of view there is a fine and intimate difference between these two ways of listening.) At this age, musical instruments are listened to far more consciously. There is also a greater understanding for the musical qualities of various instruments. Whereas earlier the instrument appeared to join in with the singing, it is now heard as a separate part. Listening and singing become two separate, though parallel, activities.

This new relationship between singing and the appreciation of the part played by musical instruments is characteristic of this new stage, and the methods of teaching must be changed accordingly. What is important is not to introduce any music theory before this age.

Music should be approached directly and any theoretical observations a teacher may wish to make should come from the students' practical experience of it. Gradually it should become possible for pupils of this age to make the transition toward forming musical judgments on a more rational basis.

What Mister Baumann indicated at the end of his contribution is absolutely correct: one can make use of the ways pupils express themselves musically to increase certain aspects of their self-knowledge. For example, in the Waldorf school we let the older students do some modeling, and from the very beginning one can perceive individual characteristics in what they produce. (When you ask children to model something or other, their work will always display distinctly individual features.) But with regard to musical activities, the teacher cannot go into the pupils' more individual characteristics until the age of sixteen or seventeen. Then, to avoid one-sidedness, it is proper to address questions presented by too much attraction toward a particular musical direction. If pupils of that age develop a passion for certain types of music—for example, if they are strongly drawn to Wagner's music (and in our times many young people slide into becoming pure Wagnerians almost automatically)—then the teacher must try to counterbalance their tendency to be too emotionally swept away by music, rather than developing an appreciation of the inner configuration of the music itself. (This in no way implies any criticism of Wagner's music.)

What happens in such a case is that the musical experience slips too easily into the emotional sphere and consequently needs to be lifted again into the realm of consciousness. A musician will notice this even in the quality of a pupil's singing voice. If music is experienced too much in the realm of feeling, the voice will sound differently from that of a young person who listens more to the formation of the tones, and who has a correct understanding of the more structural element in music.

To work toward a balanced musical feeling and understanding is particularly important at this age. Of course, the teacher, who is still the authority, does not yet have an opportunity to work in this way before the student reaches puberty. After puberty, the teacher's authority no longer counts, but the weight of the teacher's musical judgments does. Until puberty, right or wrong is concurrent with what the teacher considers to be right or wrong. After puberty reasons have to be given—musical reasons also. Therefore it is very important to go deeply into the motivation of one's own musical judgments if there is an opportunity for continuing music lessons at this age. The whole night could be spent talking about this theme, if one wished to.

Question: Is there not an element of dishonesty in asking a child a question if one knows the answer?

RUDOLF STEINER: There is something very interesting at the bottom of this question. Usually, if I ask a question it is because I want to find an answer to something I don't know. If I now question a child—knowing the answer—I commit an untruth. However, in teaching there are always imponderables to be reckoned with, and sometimes it becomes necessary to become clear about this point.

To do that, I often use the following example: If, as a teacher, one wants to speak about the question of immortality in a religious and imaginative way, one might choose the following procedure, and say to oneself: Since children cannot yet comprehend conceptual thoughts, I will use an image to convey the idea of the soul's immortality. As the teacher, I am the one who knows, and my students are uninformed. From my knowledge I will create a picture for them and say, "Look at a cocoon. When the time is right it opens, and a beautiful butterfly flies out. And just as the butterfly flies out of the cocoon, so the immortal soul flies out of the body when a human being dies." This is one way to approach the subject. Fine; but if such is one's attitude, one may find that the chosen image does not make a deep impression in the children at all. This is because the teacher, with all ingenuity, does not believe the truth of this image, which is used only to illustrate the issue of immortality to "uninformed" children.

But there is another possibility as well—that the teacher believes the truth of this picture. Then one's attitude could be: Despite my limited knowledge and wisdom, I am aware of what is real in the world, and I do believe the truth of this image. I know that I did not invent it, but that it was placed in the world through the powers that ordained the world. Through the butterfly creeping from the cocoon, what happens when the immortal human soul leaves the body is represented on a lower level, but in sense-perceptible form. And I can and do believe in this revelation.

Notice the difference: If teachers believe in the truth of their images and the words used to describe them, their inner attitude will communicate itself to the students. Innumerable examples of this can be found. And so, similarly, imponderables play into the interesting question just raised. It's not important that, as the teacher, one has the opinion: I know my subject, the child does not know it; now I will ask my question, pretending that I want to hear the answer to something I do not know. It does make a great difference, after all, whether I ask the child a question, for example, about the Battle of Zabern, and I know the answer but the child does not, or whether I know the answer and the child also knows it. The untruth would be in asking something I already know. But I could also have a different attitude—that is, I am interested in *how* the child answers the question. I may phrase my question to find out what the child feels and thinks about a particular point. In this case I don't know in advance what the child will say. The child's answer could have many different shades or nuances.

Let's assume that the teacher's ideal attitude—something I have often emphasized in my lectures—is that even the wisest is not beyond the capacity to learn, even from a tiny baby. For, no matter how far one may have advanced in scientific knowledge, a baby's cry can still teach one very much. If this is the ideal, the way a child answers each question will help teachers learn how to teach. If teachers ask questions, it does not imply that they want to hear something from their pupils that they already know, but that they themselves want to learn from the way a child answers. They will then also phrase their questions properly. For example, they may formulate a question like this: What does this mean to you? Even the tone of voice may indicate the teacher's interest in how the child will answer.

It is a fact that much depends on the imponderables that affect what happens between teacher and child. If what is going on in the child's subconscious is known, one will also discover many other things. The whole question of untruth in the teacher is part of this theme also—that is, what we find when teachers stand before their classes teaching from books or written notes. It can certainly be very convenient for them, but such expediency has a very devastating effect on the actual teaching. This is because, in their subconscious, the children are continually forming the judgment: Why should we be made to learn what even teachers do not know? Why are we made to know what they are reading from their books? This is an even greater untruth that enters the classroom than if teachers ask questions. Even when dictating, teachers should avoid doing so from books. If one perceives what is happening in the child, and if the child can feel the teacher's genuine interest in the pupils, and thus not asking questions with false undertones, the whole situation is entirely different. Then teachers can safely ask their questions without fear of introducing an element of untruth into their lessons.

Lecture Six

DORNACH, APRIL 20, 1923

Questions of ethical and social education are raised when we consider the relationship between growing children and their surroundings. We will consider these two issues today—even though briefly and superficially, due to the shortness of time. Once again, the kernel of the matter is knowing how to adapt to the individuality of the growing child. At the same time, you must remember that, as a teacher and educator, you are part of the social setting, and that you personally bring the social environment and its ethical attitudes to the growing pupil. Again, pedagogical principles and methods must be formed so that they offer every opportunity of reaching the child's true nature—one must learn to know the child's true nature according to what has been shown here briefly during the last few days. As always, much depends on *how* one's material is brought to the students during their various ages and stages.

Here we need to consider three human virtues—concerning, on the one hand, the child's own development, and on the other hand, what is seen in relation to society in general. They are three fundamental virtues. The first concerns everything that can live in *will to gratitude*; the second, everything that can live in the *will to love*; and third, everything that can live in the *will to duty.* Fundamentally, these are the three principal human virtues and, to a certain extent, encompass all other virtues.

Generally speaking, people are far too unaware of what, in this context, I would like to term gratitude or thankfulness. And yet gratitude is a virtue that, in order to play a proper role in the human soul, must grow with the child. Gratitude is something that must already flow into the human being when the growth forces—working in the child in an inward direction—are liveliest, when they are at the peak of their shaping and molding activities. Gratitude is something that has to be developed out of the bodily-religious relationship I described as the dominant feature in the child from birth until the change of teeth. At the same time, however, gratitude will develop very spontaneously during this first period of life, as long as the child is treated properly. All that flows, with devotion and love, from a child's inner being toward whatever comes from the periphery through the parents or other educators—and everything expressed outwardly in the child's imitation—will be permeated with a natural mood of gratitude. We only have to act in ways that are worthy of the child's gratitude and it will flow toward us, especially during the first period of life. This gratitude then develops further by flowing into the forces of growth that make the limbs grow, and that alter even the chemical composition of the blood and other bodily fluids. This gratitude lives in the physical body and must dwell in it, since it would not otherwise be anchored deeply enough.

It would be very incorrect to remind children constantly to be thankful for whatever comes from their surroundings. On the contrary, an atmosphere of gratitude should grow naturally in children through merely witnessing the gratitude that their elders feel as they receive what is freely given by their fellow human beings, and in how they express their gratitude. In this situation, one would also cultivate the habit of feeling grateful by allowing the child to imitate what is done in the surroundings. If a child says "thank you" very naturally—not in response to the urging of others, but simply by imitation—something has been done that will greatly benefit the child's whole life. Out of this an all-embracing gratitude will develop toward the whole world.

The cultivation of this universal gratitude toward the world is of paramount importance. It does not always need to be in one's consciousness, but may simply live in the background of the feeling life, so that, at the end of a strenuous day, one can experience gratitude, for example, when entering a beautiful meadow full of flowers. Such a subconscious feeling of gratitude may arise in us whenever we look at nature. It may be felt every morning when the Sun rises, when beholding any of nature's phenomena. And if we only act properly in front of the children, a corresponding increase in gratitude will develop within them for all that comes to them from the people living around them, from the way they speak or smile, or the way such people treat them.

This universal mood of gratitude is the basis for a truly religious attitude; for it is not always recognized that this universal sense of gratitude, provided it takes hold of the whole human being during the first period of life, will engender something even further. In human life, love flows into everything if only the proper conditions present themselves for development. The possibility of a more intense experience of love, reaching the physical level, is given only during the second period of life between the change of teeth and puberty. But that first tender love, so deeply embodied in the inner being of the child, without as yet working outward—this tender blossom will become firmly rooted through the development of gratitude. Love, born out of the experience of gratitude during the first period of the child's life, is the love of God. One should realize that, just as one has to dig the roots of a plant into the soil in order to receive its blossom later on, one also has to plant gratitude into the soul of the child, because it is the root of the love of God. The love of God will develop out of universal gratitude, as the blossom develops from the root.

We should attend to these things, because in the abstract we usually know very well how they should be. In actual life situations, however, all too often these things turn out to be very different. It is easy enough, in theory, to say that people should carry the love of God within themselves—and this could not be more correct. But such demands, made abstractly, have a peculiar habit of never seeing the light of day in practice.

I would like to return to what I said during one of the last few days. It is easy enough to think of the function of a stove in the following way: You are a stove and we have to put you here because we want to heat the room. Your categorical imperative—the true categorical "stove-imperative"—tells you that you are obliged to heat the room. We know only too well that this in itself will not make the slightest difference in the temperature of the room. But we can also save our sermonizing, and, instead, simply light the stove and heat it with suitable logs. Then it will radiate its warmth without being reminded of its categorical imperative. And this is how it is when, during various stages of childhood, we bring the right thing to children at the right time. If, during the first period of life, we create an atmosphere of gratitude around children, and if we do something else, of which I shall speak later, then, out of this gratitude toward the world, toward the entire universe, and also out of an inner thankfulness for being in this world at all (which is something that should ensoul all people), the most deep-seated and warmest piety will grow. Not the kind that lives on one's lips or in thought only, but piety that will pervade the entire human being, that will be upright, honest, and true. As for gratitude, it must grow; but this can happen with the intensity necessary for such a soul and spiritual quality only when it develops from the child's tender life-stirrings during the time from birth to its change of teeth. And then this gratitude will become the root of the love of God. It is the foundation for the love of God.

Knowing all this will make us realize that, when we receive children into the first grade, we must also consider the kinds of lives they have led before reaching school age. There should really be direct contact with the parental home—that is, with what has happened before the child entered school. This contact should always be worked for, because teachers should have a fairly clear picture of how the present situation of children was influenced by their social conditions and the milieu in which they grew up. At school, teachers will then find plenty of opportunities to rectify any possible hindrances. For this to happen, however, knowledge of the child's home background, through contact with the parents, is of course absolutely essential. It is necessary that teachers can observe how certain characteristics have developed in a child by simply watching and imitating the mother at home. To be aware of this is very important when the child begins schooling. It is just as much part of teaching as what is done in the classroom. These matters must not be overlooked if one wants to build an effective and properly based education.

We have already seen that, in the years between the child's change of teeth and the coming of puberty, the development of a sense for the authority of the teacher is both natural and essential. The second fundamental virtue, which is love, then grows from that when the child is in the process of also developing the physical basis of love. But one must see love in its true light, for, because of the prevailing materialistic attitudes of our time, the concept of love has become very one-sided and narrow; and because a materialistic outlook tends to see love only in terms of sexual love, it generally traces all manifestations of love back to a hidden sexuality. In an instance of what I called "amateurism squared" the day before yesterday, we find, if not in every case, that at least many psychologists trace human traits back to sexual origins, even if they have nothing whatsoever to do with sex. To balance such an attitude, the teacher must have acquired at least some degree of appreciation for the universal nature of love; for sexual love is not the only thing that begins to develop between the child's second dentition and puberty, but also love in its fullest sense, love for everything in the world. Sexual love is only one aspect of love that develops at this time of life. At that age one can see how love of nature and love for fellow human beings awaken in the child, and the teacher needs to have a strong view of how sexual love represents only one facet, one single chapter in life's book of love. If one realizes this, one will also know how to assign sexual love to its proper place in life. Today, for many people who look at life with theoretical eyes, sexual love has become a kind of Moloch who devours his own offspring, inasmuch as, if such views were true, sexual love would devour all other forms of love.

The way love develops in the human soul is different from the way gratitude does. Gratitude has to grow with the growing human being, and this is why it has to be planted when the child's growing forces are at their strongest. Love, on the other hand, has to *awaken*. The development of love really does resemble the process of awakening, and, like awakening, it has to remain more in the region of the soul. The gradual emergence of love is a slow awakening, until the final stage of this process has been reached. Observe for a moment what happens when one awakes in the morning. At first there is a dim awareness of vague notions; perhaps first sensations begin to stir;

slowly the eyelids struggle free of being closed; gradually the outer world aids one's awakening; and finally the moment arrives when that awakening passes into the physical body.

This is also how it is with the awakening of love—except that, in the child, this process takes about seven years. At first love begins to stir when sympathy is aroused for whatever is taught during the early days at school. If we begin to approach the child with the kind of imagery I have described, we can see how love especially comes to meet this activity. Everything has to be saturated with this love. At that stage, love has a profoundly soul-like and tender quality. If one compares it with the daily process of waking up, one would still be deeply asleep, or at least in a state of sleeping-dreaming. (Here I am referring to the child's condition, of course—the teacher must not be in a dream, although this appears to happen all too often!) This condition then yields to a stronger jolt into wakefulness. And in what I described yesterday and the day before about the ninth and tenth years—and especially in the time leading up to the twelfth year—love of nature awakens in the child. Only then do we see it truly emerging.

Before this stage, the child's relationship to nature is completely different. A child then has a great love for all that belongs to the fairyworld of nature, a love that has to be nourished by a creative and pictorial approach. Love for the realities in nature awakens only later. At this point we are faced with a particularly difficult task. Into everything connected with the curriculum at this time of life (causality, the study of lifeless matter, an understanding of historical interconnections, the beginnings of physics and chemistry) into all of this, the teacher must introduce—and here I am not joking, but speak very earnestly—the teacher must introduce an element of *grace*. In geometry or physics lessons, for example, there is every need for the teacher to allow real grace to enter into teaching. All lessons should be pervaded with an air of graciousness, and, above all, the subjects must never be allowed to become sour. So often, just during the ages from eleven and a half, or eleven and three-quarters, to fourteen or fifteen, work in these subjects suffers so much by becoming unpalatable and sour. What the pupils have to learn about the refraction and reflection of light or about the measurement of surface areas in a spherical calotte, is so often spoken of not with grace, but with an air of sourness.

At just this time of life the teacher must remember the need for a certain "soul-breathing" in the lessons, which communicates itself to the pupils in a very strange way—soul-breathing must be allowed for. Ordinary breathing consists of inhaling and exhaling. In most cases, or at least on many occasions, teachers, in their physics and geometry lessons, only breathe out with their souls. They do not breathe in, and the out-breath is what produces this acidity. I am referring to the out-breathing of soul expressed in dull and monotonous descriptions, which infuses all content with the added seriousness of inflated proportion. Seriousness does have its place, but not through exaggeration.

On the other hand, an in-breathing of soul brings an inherent sense of humor that is always prepared to sparkle, both within and outside the classroom, or whenever an opportunity arises for teachers and pupils to be together. The only possible hindrance to such radiating humor is the teachers themselves. The children certainly would not stand in its way, nor would the various subjects, provided they were handled with just the right touch during this particular age. If teachers could feel at home in their subjects to the degree that they were entirely free of having to chew over their content while presenting lessons, then they might find themselves in a position where even reflected light is likely to crack a joke, or where a spherical skullcap might calculate its surface area with a winning smile. Of course, jokes should not be planned ahead, nor should they be forced on the classroom situation. Everything should be tinted with spontaneous humor, which is inherent within the content, and not artificially grafted onto it. This is the core of the matter. Humor has to be found in things themselves and, above all, it should not even be necessary to search for it. At best, teachers who have prepared their lessons properly need to bring a certain order and discipline into the ideas that will come to them while teaching, for this is what happens if one is well prepared. The opposite is equally possible, however, if one has not prepared the lessons adequately; one will feel deprived of ideas because one still has to wrestle with the lesson content. This spoils a healthy out-breathing of soul and shuts out the humor-filled air it needs. These are the important points one has to remember at this particular age.

If teaching follows its proper course in this way, the awakening of love will happen so that the student's soul and spirit are properly integrated into the human organization during the final stage of this awakening—that is, when the approach of puberty, begins. This is when what first developed so tenderly in the child's soul, and then in a more robust way, can finally take hold of the bodily nature in the right and proper way.

Now you may wonder what teachers have to do to be capable of accomplishing their tasks as described. Here we have to consider something I would like to call the "social aspect" of the teaching profession, the importance of which is recognized far too little. Too often we encounter an image that a certain era (not ancient times, however) has associated with the teaching profession, whose members are not generally respected and honored as they should be. Only when society looks upon teachers with the respect their calling deserves, only when it recognizes that the teachers stand at the forefront of bringing new impulses into our civilization—not just in speeches from a political platform—only then will teachers receive the moral support they need to do their work. Such an attitude—or perhaps better still, such a sentiment—would pave the way toward acquiring a wider and more comprehensive view of life. This is what the teachers need; they also need to be fully integrated into life. They need more than just the proper qualifications in educational principles and methods, more than just special training for their various subjects; most of all teachers need something that will renew itself again and again: a view of life that pulsates in a living way through their souls. What they need is a deep understanding of life itself; they need far more than what can pass from their lips as they stand in front of their classes. All of this has to flow into the making of a teacher. Strictly speaking, the question of education should be part of the social question, and it must embrace not just the actual teaching schools, but also the inner development of the teaching faculty.

It should be understood, at the same time, that the aims and aspirations for contemporary education, as presented here, are in no way rebellious or revolutionary. To believe that would be a great misunderstanding. What is advocated here can be introduced into the present situation without any need for radical changes. And yet, one feels tempted to add that it is just this social aspect of education that points to so many topical questions in life. And so, I would like to mention something, not because I want to agitate against present conditions, but only to illustrate, to put into words, what is bound to come one day. It will not happen in our current age, so please do not view what I am going to say as something radical or revolutionary.

As you know, it is customary today to confer a doctorate on people who, fundamentally speaking, have not yet gained any practical experience in the subjects for which they are given their degree, whether chemistry, geography, or geology. And yet, the proof of their knowledge and capacity would surely have to include the ability to pass their expertise on to other candidates, of teaching them.[1] And so a doctor's degree should not really be granted until a candidate has passed the practical test of teaching and training others who wish to take up the same vocation. You can see great wisdom, based on instinctive knowledge, in the popular expression; for, in the vernacular, only a person capable of healing, capable of giving tangible proof of healing abilities, is called a "doctor." In this instance the word *doctor* refers to someone engaged as a practical healer, and not just to a person who has acquired specialized medical knowledge, however comprehensive this might be.

Two concepts have arisen gradually from the original single concept—that of educating as well as that of healing. In more distant times, teaching or educating was also thought of as including healing. The process of educating was considered synonymous with that of healing. Because it was felt that the human being bore too many marks of physical heredity, education was viewed as a form of healing, as I have already mentioned during a previous meeting here. Using the terminology of past ages, one could even say teaching was considered a means of healing the effects of original sin.[2] Seen in this light, the processes of healing, set in motion by the doctor, are fundamentally the same as those of teaching, though in a different realm of life. From a broader perspective, the teacher is as much of a healer as a doctor. And so the weight the title "doctor" usually carries in the eyes of the public could well become dependent on a general awareness that only those who have

1. The word *doctor* is derived from *docere*, the Latin verb meaning "to teach." — TRANS.
2. See footnote on page 37.

passed the test of practical experience should receive the honor of the degree. Otherwise, this title would remain only a label.

However, as I have already said, this must not be misunderstood as the demand of an instigator for the immediate present. I would not even have mentioned it except in a pedagogical context. I am only too aware of the kind of claims that are likely to be listened to in our times, and the ones that inevitably give the impression one is trying to crash through closed doors. If one wants to accomplish something in life, one must be willing to forgo abstract aims or remote ideals, the attempted realization of which would either break one's neck or bruise one's forehead. One must always try to remain in touch with reality. Then one is also justified in using something to illustrate certain needs of our time, even if these may only be fulfilled in the future; for what I have spoken of cannot be demanded for a very long time to come. It may help us to appreciate, nevertheless, the dignity within the social sphere that should be due the teaching profession. I have mentioned all of this because it seemed important that we should see this question in the proper light. If teachers can feel moral support coming from society as a whole, then the gradual awakening of love in the young will become the close ally of their natural sense of authority, which must prevail in schools. Such things sometimes originate in very unexpected places.

Just as the love of God is rooted in gratitude, so genuine moral impulses originate in love, as was described. For nothing else can be the basis for truly ethical virtue except a kind of love for humankind that does not allow us to pass our fellow human beings without bothering to know them, because we no longer have an eye for what lives in them—as happens so easily nowadays. The general love toward all people is the love that reaches out for human understanding everywhere. It is the love that awakens in the child in the time between the change of teeth and puberty, just as gratitude has grown between the child's birth and the loss of the first teeth. At school, we must do everything we can to awaken love.

How are children affected by what happens in their immediate surroundings during the first period of life—that is, from birth to the change of teeth? They see that people engage in all kinds of activities. But what children take in are not the actual accomplishments in themselves, for they have not yet developed the faculty to perceive them consciously. What they do perceive are meaningful gestures. During this first period of life we are concerned with only a childlike understanding of the meaningful gestures they imitate. And from the perception of these meaningful gestures the feeling of gratitude develops, from which the gratitude-engendered will to act arises.

Nor do children perceive the activities happening in their environment during the subsequent years, between the change of teeth and puberty—especially not during the early stages of this period. What they do perceive—even in the kinds of movements of the people around them—no longer represents the sum total of meaningful gestures. Instead, events begin to speak to the children, become a meaningful language. Not just what is spoken in actual words, but every physical movement and every activity speaks directly to the child during this particular time. It makes all the difference, therefore, whether a teacher writes on the blackboard:

Leaf

Or writes the same word thus:

Leaf

Whether the teacher writes the figure seven like this:

$$7$$

Or like this:

$$7$$

Whether it is written in an artistic, in a less-refined, or even in a slovenly way, makes a great difference. The way in which these things affect the child's life is what matters. Whether the word *leaf* is written in the first or second way (see above), is a meaningful language for the child. Whether the teacher enters the classroom in a dignified manner, or whether the teacher tries to cut a fine figure, speaks directly to the child. Likewise, whether the teacher is always fully awake to the classroom situation—this will show itself in the child's eye by the way the teacher handles various objects during the lessons—or, during wintertime, whether it could even happen that the teacher absent-mindedly walks off with the blackboard towel around his or her neck, mistaking it for a scarf—all of this speaks volumes to the child. It is not so much the outer actions that work on the child, but what lives behind them, whether unpleasant and ugly, or charming and pleasant.

In this context, it is even possible that a certain personal habit of a teacher may generate a friendly atmosphere in the classroom, even if it might appear, in itself, very comic. For example, from my thirteenth to eighteenth year I had a teacher—and I always considered him to be my best teacher—who never began a lesson without gently blowing his nose first. Had he ever started his lesson without doing so, we would have sorely missed it. I am not saying that he was at all conscious of the effect this was having on his pupils, but one really begins to wonder whether in such a case it would even be right to expect such a person to overcome an ingrained habit. But this is an altogether different matter. I have mentioned this episode only as an illustration.

The point is, everything teachers do in front of children at this stage of life constitutes meaningful language for them. The actual words that teachers speak are merely part of this language. There are many other unconscious factors lying in the depths of the feeling life that also play a part. For example, the child has an extraordinarily fine perception (which never reaches the sphere of consciousness) of whether a teacher makes up to one or another pupil during lessons or whether she or he behaves in a natural and dignified way. All this is of immense importance to the child. In addition, it makes a tremendous difference to the pupils whether teachers have prepared themselves well enough to present their lessons without having to use printed or written notes, as already mentioned during our discussion. Without being aware of it, children ask themselves: Why should I have to know what the teachers do not know? After all, I too am only human. Teachers are supposed to be fully grown up, and I am only a child. Why should I have to work so hard to learn what even they don't know?

This is the sort of thing that deeply torments the child's unconscious, something that cannot be rectified once it has become fixed there. It confirms that the sensitive yet natural relationship between teachers and students of this age can come about only if the teachers—forgive this rather pedantic remark, but it cannot be avoided in this situation—have the subject completely at their fingertips. It must live "well-greased" in them— if I may use this expression—but not in the sense of bad and careless writing.[3] I use it here in the sense of

---

3. In German, "very untidy writing" is often referred to as *Geschmier,* a "smear on the page." The verb *schmieren* also means "to grease." — TRANS.

greasing wheels to make them run smoothly. Teachers will then feel in full command of the classroom situation, and they will act accordingly. This in itself will ensure an atmosphere where it would never occur to students to be impudent.

For that to happen among children of ten, eleven, or twelve would really be one of the worst possible things. We must always be aware that whatever we say to our pupils, even if we are trying to be humorous, should never induce them to give a frivolous or insolent reply. An example of this is the following situation: A teacher might say to a student who suddenly got stuck because of a lack of effort and attention, "Here the ox stands held up by the mountain." And the pupil retorts, "Sir, I am not a mountain."[4] This sort of thing must not be allowed to happen. If the teachers have prepared their lessons properly, a respectful attitude will emerge toward them as a matter of course. And if such an attitude is present, such an impertinent reply would be unthinkable. It may, of course, be of a milder and less undermining kind. I have mentioned it only to illustrate my point. Such impudent remarks would destroy not only the mood for work in the class, but they could easily infect other pupils and thus spoil a whole class.

Only when the transition from the second life period to the third occurs, is the possibility given for (how shall I call them now in these modern times?) young men and young women to observe the activities occurring around them. Previously the meaningful gesture was perceived, and later the meaningful language of the events around the child. Only now does the possibility exist for the adolescent to observe the activities performed

---

4. The German saying "*Wie der Ochs Corm Berg stehen.*" It means literally "to stand there like the ox facing the mountain." It is a very common saying, and it can also be translated as "to be completely out of one's depth," "to be nonplussed." — TRANS.

by other people in the environment. I have also said that, by perceiving meaningful gestures, and through experiencing gratitude, the love for God develops, and that, through the meaningful language that comes from the surroundings, love for everything human is developed as the foundation for an individual sense of morality. If now the adolescent is enabled to observe other people's activities properly, love of work will develop. While gratitude must be allowed to grow, and love must be awakened, what needs to evolve now must appear with the young person's full inner awareness. We must have enabled the young person to enter this new phase of development after puberty with full inner awareness, so that in a certain way the adolescent comes to find the self. Then love of work will develop. This love of work has to grow freely on the strength of what has already been attained. This is love of work in general and also love for what one does oneself. At the moment when an understanding for the activities of other people awakens as a complementary image, a conscious attitude toward love of work, a love of "doing" must arise. In this way, during the intervening stages, the child's early play has become transmuted into the proper view of work, and this is what we must aim for in our society today.

What part do teachers and educators have to play in all of this? This is something that belongs to one of the most difficult things in their vocational lives. For the best thing teachers can do for the child during the first and second life period is to help what will awaken on its own with the beginning of puberty. When, to their everlasting surprise, teachers witness time and again how the child's individuality is gradually emerging, they have to realize that they themselves have been only a tool. Without this attitude, sparked by this realization, one can hardly be a proper teacher; for in classes one is faced with the most varied types of individuals, and it would never do to stand in the classroom with the feeling that all of one's students should become copies of oneself. Such a sentiment should never arise—and why not? Because it could very well happen that, if one is fortunate enough, among the pupils there might be three or four budding geniuses, very distinct from the dull ones, about whom we will have more to say later. Surely you will acknowledge that it is not possible to select only geniuses for the teaching profession, that it is certain that teachers are not endowed with the genius that some of their students will display in later life. Yet teachers must be able to educate not only pupils of their own capacity, but also those who, with their exceptional brightness, will far outshine them.

However, teachers will be able to do this only if they get out of the habit of hoping to make their pupils into what they themselves are. If they can make a firm resolve to stand in the school as selflessly as possible, to obliterate not only their own sympathies and antipathies, but also their personal ambitions, in order to dedicate themselves to whatever comes from the students, then they will properly educate potential geniuses as well as the less-bright pupils. Only such an attitude will lead to the realization that *all education is, fundamentally, a matter of self-education.*

Essentially, there is no education other than self-education, whatever the level may be. This is recognized in its full depth within anthroposophy, which has conscious knowledge through spiritual investigation of repeated Earth lives. Every education is self-education, and as teachers we can only provide the environment for children's self-education. We have to provide the most favorable conditions where, through our agency, children can educate themselves according to their own destinies.

This is the attitude that teachers should have toward children, and such an attitude can be developed only through an ever-growing awareness of this fact. For people in general there may be many kinds of prayers. Over and above these there is this special prayer for the teacher:

> Dear God, cause that I—inasmuch as my personal ambitions are concerned—negate myself. And Christ make true in me the Pauline words, "Not I, but the Christ in me."

This prayer, addressed to God in general and to Christ in particular, continues: "... so that the Holy Spirit may hold sway in the teacher." This is the true Trinity.

If one can live in these thoughts while in close proximity to the students, then the hoped-for results of this education can also become a social act at the same time. But other matters also come into play, and I can only touch on them. Just consider what, in the opinion of many people, would have to be done to improve today's social order. People expect better conditions through the implementation of external measures. You need only look at the dreadful experiments being carried out in Soviet Russia. There the happiness of the whole world is sought through the inauguration of external programs. It is believed that improvements in the social sphere depend on the creation of institutions. And yet, these are the least significant factors within social development. You can set up any institutions you like, be they monarchist or republican, democratic or socialist; the decisive factor will always be the kind of people who live and work under any of these systems. For those who spread a socializing influence, the two things that matter are a loving devotion toward what they are doing, and an understanding interest in what others are doing.

Think about what can flow from just these two attributes; at least people can work together again in the social sphere. But this will have to become a tradition over ages. As long as you merely work externally, you will produce no tangible results. You have to bring out these two qualities from the depths of human nature. If you want to introduce changes by external means, even when established with the best of intentions, you will find that people will not respond as expected. And, conversely, their actions may elude your understanding. Institutions are the outcome of individual endeavor. You can see this everywhere. They were created by the very two qualities that more or less lived in the initiators—that is, loving devotion toward what they were doing, and an understanding interest in what others were doing.

When one looks at the social ferment in our times with open eyes, one finds that the strangest ideas have arisen, especially in the social sphere, simply because the current situation was not understood properly. Let me give you an example:

Today, the message of so-called Marxism regarding human labor and its relationship to social classes is being drummed not just into thousands but into millions of heads.[5] And if you investigate what its author alleges to have discovered—something with which millions of people are being indoctrinated so that they see it as their socialist gospel, to use as a means for political agitation—you will find it all based upon a fundamental error regarding the attitude toward social realities. Karl Marx wants to base the value of work on the human energy spent performing it.[6] This leads to a complete absurdity, because, from the perspective of energy output, it makes no difference whether someone cuts a certain quantity of firewood within a given time, or whether—if one can afford to avoid such a menial task—one expends the same energy and time on

5. See Karl Marx's major work, *Das Kapital* (*Capital*), *Vol.* I, Hamburg, 1867.
6. Karl Heinrich Marx (1818–1883), German political philosopher and co-author, with Friedrich Engels, of *The Communist Manifesto* in 1848.

treading the pedals of a wheel specially designed to combat incipient obesity. According to Karl Marx's reckoning, there is no difference between the human energy expended on those two physical activities. But cutting firewood has its proper place within the social order. Treading the pedals of a slimming cycle, on the other hand, is of no social use, because it only produces a hygienic effect for the person doing it. And yet, Karl Marx's yardstick for measuring the value of work consists of calculating the food consumption necessary for work to be done. This way of assessing the value of labor within the context of the national economy is simply absurd. Nevertheless, all kinds of calculations were made toward this end. The importance of one factor, however, was ignored—that is, *loving devotion toward what one is doing* and *an understanding interest in what others are doing.*

What we must achieve when we are with young people is that, through our own conduct, a full consciousness of the social implications contained in those two things will enter the minds of adolescents. To do so we must realize what it means to stand by children so that we can aid in their own self-education.

Lecture Seven

As you can probably imagine, it is not easy for one who is free from a fanatical or sectarian attitude to accomplish the kind of education, based on knowledge of the human being, that we have spoken of in the past few days. Many of you will have noticed already that what is considered here to be both right and good in education differs in many ways from what is found in conventional forms of education, with their regulations, curricula, and other fundamental policies. In this respect, one finds oneself caught in a dilemma.

On the one hand, we stand on the firm ground of a pedagogy that derives from objective knowledge, and that prescribes specific curricular and educational tasks for each year (as you will have discovered already from what you have heard so far). To ascertain what must be done in this education, we take our cue from the children themselves; and not only for each year, but also for each month, each week, and, in the end, each day. Here I feel justified in expressing appreciation for how much the teachers of the Waldorf schools have responded to the objective demands of a truly grounded pedagogy, and also for their insight into how this pedagogy is related to the needs of the growing child.[1] They have come to realize that not a single detail of this pedagogy is arbitrary, that everything in it is a direct response to what can be read in the child's own nature. This represents one side of what has led to the dilemma. The other side consists of demands made by life itself. Those who are free of any fanaticism despite their own ideals (or whatever else you choose to call these things), and who feel the need for firm roots in life's realities, experience this other aspect with particular acuity.

Sectarianism to any degree or fanatical zeal must never be allowed to creep into our educational endeavors, only to find at the end of the road that our students do not fit into life as it is; for life in the world does not notice one's educational ideals. Life is governed by what arises from the prevailing conditions themselves, which are expressed as regulations concerning education, as school curricula, and as other related matters, which correspond to current ways of thinking. And so there is always a danger that we will educate children in a way that, though correct in itself, could alienate them from life in the world—whether one considers this right or wrong. It must always be remembered that one must not steer fanatically toward one's chosen educational aims without considering whether or not one might be alienating one's students from surrounding life.

Opponents of anthroposophy have often attributed fanaticism and sectarianism to this movement, but this is not the case, as you will see. On the contrary, it is precisely these two attributes that are alien to its nature. They may appear within some individual members, but anthroposophy itself always

---

1. In August and September 1919, Rudolf Steiner gave three courses to the teachers of the first Waldorf school, which was founded by the industrialist Emil Molt for the children of the workers in his cigarette factory, and which was opened on September 7, 1919.

strives to enter fully into the realities of life. And just because of this, one is only too aware of the difficulties encountered in dealing with the practical sides of life. From the very beginning of the Waldorf school something had to be done. It is difficult to give it a proper name, but something bad or negative had to be agreed upon—that is, a kind of compromise—simply because this school is not grounded in fanaticism but in objective reality. At the very beginning, a memorandum addressed to the local school authorities had to be worked out. In it I made the following points: During the first three years the students in our school are to be educated, stage by stage and wherever possible, according to what is considered relevant to their inner needs. At the same time, the standards generally achieved in other schools are to be respected to the extent that, after completion of the first three years, the students of the Waldorf school should be able to fulfill the necessary requirements for entering corresponding classes in other schools, if desired. Such an offer, for our teachers, amounted to an "ingratiating compromise"—forgive this term, I cannot express it otherwise. A realistic mind has to take such a course, for discretion is essential in everything one does. A fanatic would have responded differently. Naturally, many difficulties have to be ironed out when such a policy is chosen, and many of our teachers would find it preferable to steer a straight course toward our aims and ideals. Lengthy and minutely detailed discussions occurred before a passage was found through these two conflicting approaches.

Another point in my memorandum was that, after completion of their twelfth year—that is, when our pupils are in the sixth grade, counting upward from the first grade—they should again be able to fulfill the requirements for entry into the corresponding class in another school. My choice for this particular age is based on the fact that it marks the end of a period of development, as already described during a previous meeting. And finally, it was presented in the memorandum that, in their fourteenth year, our students should have reached again the necessary standards of learning that would enable them, if desired, to change schools.

In retrospect, one could say that during the first three grades this plan has worked fairly well. At that level it has been tolerably successful. With a great deal of effort and trouble, it is still workable until the students' twelfth year. However, the real difficulties begin during the following years, for out of a dark subconsciousness, some knowledge of what is happening in a young child lingered from the distant past into our present time, however dim this insight may have become today. And because of this it is now customary to send children to school when they are losing their first teeth. Today people hardly realize that these two things are connected. Nevertheless, entering school at about six is still the result of ancient wisdom, passed on through the ages, which today has become only vague and instinctive. Since these things are no longer recognized, however, there is a tendency toward arbitrarily establishing the age for entering school at the completion of the sixth year, which is always a little premature, and therefore not in keeping with the child's nature. There is nothing one can do about it, because if parents do not send their children to school when they have completed their sixth year, the police or bailiff, or whatever else such people are called, will come and take the children to school.

However, as previously mentioned, it is relatively easy to work with this compromise during the first three years. Admittedly, if one or another student has to leave the Waldorf school for another school during this time because of circumstance, one is usually told that such students are behind in reading and writing. They may be considered far ahead in artistic subjects, such as in drawing or eurythmy, but these, so we are told, are not generally considered to be very important.

Such official judgments, however, can even be seen as an affirmation of Waldorf methods! They prompt me to tell you something interesting about the young Goethe.[2] If you look at his spelling, even when he was much older than seven or eight, you will find it full of atrocious mistakes. It is easy to deduce from this that far more is expected of an eight-year-old child today (if "more" is the right word) than what Goethe managed to achieve at seventeen (only with regard to spelling, of course). This certainly demonstrates that there is also another way of judging the situation, for Goethe owed much to the fact that, even at the age of seventeen, he was still likely to make spelling errors because, not having been too fettered to rigid rules, his inner being could remain flexible with regard to the unfolding of certain soul forces. If one knows how these things interact with each other (and a more sensitive kind of psychology is needed for this than is frequently encountered today) one will be no more influenced by adverse criticism than by the superficial criteria of such a historical fact, which is interesting, at least.

Another interesting example can be found in so-called *Mendelisms*, which emerged around the beginning of the twentieth century (perhaps even around the end of the nineteenth century), and which was considered by natural scientists to be the best theory for explaining the phenomena of heredity. It received its name from a certain Gregor Mendel,[3] a botanist who lived during the middle of the nineteenth century and was

---

2. Johann Wolfgang von Goethe (1749–1832) German poet, scientist, and philosopher.
3. Gregor Johann Mendel (1822–1884) Austrian botanist. He became a monk in the order of Saint Augustine in 1843, and taught in a technical school from 1854 until 1868, when he became abbot. He is known for his experiments in breeding peas in the monastery garden, and from the statistics gathered, he established certain laws concerning heredity, which became the foundation of the science of genetics.

also a teacher at a *Realschule* in Moravia.[4] Gregor Mendel made careful experiments with plants in order to investigate their inherited properties. His writings remained obscure for a long time, only to surface again toward the turn of the century, to be hailed as the most convincing theory regarding heredity.

Now it is interesting to consider the biography of Gregor Mendel. As our Austrian friends here know, monastic clerics had to pass an examination before they could become eligible for a teaching post at a high school. Mendel failed his exam brilliantly, which meant that he was considered incapable of becoming a high school teacher. But an Austrian regulation existed permitting failed candidates to retake their exams after a certain period of time. Gregor Mendel did so and again failed spectacularly. I believe that even today in Austria such a person could never find a high school teaching position. In those days, however, regulations were a little less stringent. Because of a shortage of teachers at the time, even failed candidates were sometimes hired as teachers, and so Gregor Mendel did finally become a high school teacher, even though he had twice failed his exam. Since this had been made possible only through the grace of the headmaster, however, he was considered to be a second-rate staff member by his colleagues and, according to the rules governing high school teachers, he was not entitled to add "Ph.D." to his name. Successful exam candidates usually write these abbreviated degrees after their names, for example, "Joseph Miller, Ph.D." In the case of Gregor Mendel these letters were missing, the omission of which indicated his inferior position. Well, several decades passed, but after his death this same individual was hailed as one of the greatest naturalists!

---

4. *Realschule* (or *Realgymnasium*) is the high school equivalent in Germany for preparation in the sciences, trades, or technical studies, whereas *Gymnasium* usually refers to a high school for classical preparation toward university study.

Real life presents some strange examples. And, although it is impossible to plan the education of young people to suit the practical demands of later life (since, if this were the only aim, some very strange requests would certainly be made), even though one cannot adapt the curricula to what life itself will bring to maturity later on, one must nevertheless be ready to listen with inner clarity and a sense of psychology to what the many occurrences in life are trying to tell us, with regard to both primary and secondary education. So it could certainly be said that it is not really a tragedy when a Waldorf student has to leave during the third grade, a student who has not yet reached the same level of achievement in certain elementary skills as students in another school, who were drilled using bad methods, the harmful effects of which will surface only later in life. Many life stories could be told to substantiate this claim. Strange things sometimes show up when one looks at obituaries. Röntgen, for example, was also excluded from teaching at a high school, and only through the special kindness of an influential person was he allowed to gain a teaching post at all.[5] As already said, one cannot base one's educational ideas on such things, but they should be noticed, and one must try to comprehend their significance through a more discriminating psychology.

Returning to our point, after the twelfth year it becomes increasingly difficult to find a workable compromise in our way of teaching. Until the twelfth year it is just possible to do so, as long as one really knows what is going on inside the students. But afterward, the situation begins to get more and more difficult, because from that time on, the curricula and the required standards for achievement no longer have any relationship to the nature of the growing human being; they are chosen

5. Wilhelm Konrad von Röntgen (1845–1923) German physicist, discoverer of the "Röntgen" rays or X-rays.

entirely arbitrarily. The subject matter to be covered in any one year is chosen entirely autocratically, and one simply can no longer bridge the conflicting demands, on the one hand, from the powers that be, and, on the other hand, those that arise directly from the evolving human being. Remember what I said yesterday: by the time puberty is passed, the adolescent should have been helped toward developing sufficient maturity and inner strength to enter the realm of human freedom. I referred to the two fundamental virtues: *gratitude*, for which the ground has to be prepared before the change of teeth, and *the ability to love*, for which the ground needs to be prepared between the change of teeth and puberty; this was the theme developed yesterday.

Furthermore, we have seen that, with regard to the ethical life, the soul life of the child must also experience feelings of sympathy and antipathy toward what is good and evil. If one approaches a student at this age with a "thou shalt" attitude, proper development will be hindered in the years to come. On the other hand, when one instead moves the pre-adolescent child, through natural authority, to love the good and hate the evil, then during the time of sexual maturity, from the inner being of the adolescent, the third fundamental virtue develops, which is the *sense of duty.* It is impossible to drill it into young people. It can only unfold as a part of natural development, based only on gratitude—in the sense described yesterday— and on the ability to love. If these two virtues have been developed properly, with sexual maturity the sense of duty will emerge, the experience of which is an essential part of life

What belongs to the human soul and spirit realm has to develop according to its own laws and conditions, just as what belongs to the physical realm must obey physical laws. Just as an arm or a hand must be allowed to grow freely, according to the inner forces of growth, just as these must not be artificially controlled by, for example, being fixed into a rigid iron frame—although in certain places on Earth there is a custom of restricting the free growth of feet similar to the way we impede the free unfolding here of the child's soul life—so must adolescents feel this new sense of duty arising freely from within. The young person will then integrate properly into society, and Goethe's dictum will find its noblest fulfillment: *"Duty is a love for what one demands of oneself."* Here again you see how love plays into everything, and how the sense of duty must be developed so that one eventually comes to love it. In this way one integrates properly as a human being into society. And then, from the previous experience of right authority, the ability to support oneself by one's own strength will evolve.

What is finally revealed as genuine piety, when seen with spiritual eyes, is the transformed body-related, natural religiousness during the time before the change of teeth, which I described to you in fair detail. These are all things that must be rooted deeply in a true pedagogy, and applied practically. Soon enough, one will realize how necessary it is to allow the curriculum—from the twelfth year until puberty, and, most of all, after puberty—to be more and more inclined toward practical activities. In the Waldorf school, the ground for this task is prepared early. In our school, boys and girls sit side by side. Although interesting psychological facts have emerged from this practice alone—and each class has its own psychology, of which we will speak more tomorrow—one can definitely say: if one lets boys and girls practice their handcrafts side by side as a matter of course, it is an excellent preparation for their adult lives. Today there are only a few men who recognize how much the ability to knit can help toward healthy thinking and healthy logic. Only a few men can judge what it means for one's life to be able to knit. In our Waldorf school, boys do their knitting alongside the girls, and they also mend socks.

Through this practice, the differentiation between the types of work performed by the two sexes will find its natural course later on, should this become necessary. At the same time, a form of education is being implemented that considers fully the practical aspects of the students' future lives.

People are always extremely surprised when they hear me say (and the following assertion not only expresses my personal conviction, but is based on a psychological fact) that I cannot consider anyone to be a good professor in the full meaning of the word unless that person can also mend a shoe in an emergency; for how could it be possible for anyone to know something of real substance about being and becoming in the world, unless that person can also repair a shoe or a boot if the situation demands it? This is, of course, a rather sweeping statement, but there are men who cannot even sew on a button properly, and this is a lamentable failing. Knowledge of philosophy carries little weight, unless one can also lend a hand to whatever needs doing. This is simply part of life. In my opinion, one can only be a good philosopher if one could have just as well become a shoemaker, should this have been one's destiny. And, as the history of philosophy shows, it sometimes happens that cobblers become philosophers.[6]

Knowledge of the human being calls on us to make adequate provision in our curricula and schedules for preparing pupils for the practical side of life. Reading in the book of human nature, we are simply led to introduce the children—or rather, the young men and women, as we should call them now—to the art of setting up a loom and weaving. From there it follows quite naturally that they should also learn to spin, and that they gain a working idea of how paper is made, for example.

---

6. For example, Jakob Böhme (1575–1624), the shoemaker from Görlitz, whose influence has been far-reaching in Western philosophical and spiritual streams.

They should be taught not only mechanics and chemistry, but also how to understand at least simple examples of mechanical and chemical processes used in technology. They should reproduce these on a small scale with their own hands so they will know how various articles are manufactured. This change of direction toward the more practical side of life must certainly be made possible. It has to be worked toward with honest and serious intent if one wants to build the proper curriculum, especially in the upper classes.

But this can place one in terrible difficulties. It is just possible to equip children under nine with sufficient learning skills for a transfer into the fourth grade of another school, without neglecting what needs to be done with them for sound pedagogical reasons. This is also still possible in the case of twelve-year-olds who are to enter the seventh grade. It is already becoming very difficult indeed to bring pupils to the required standards of learning for their transfer to a high school. Tremendous difficulties have to be overcome if pupils from our higher grades have to change to a high school.

In such cases one would do well to recall ancient Greece, where a wise Greek had to put up with being told by an Egyptian, "You Greeks are like children—you know nothing about all the changes the Earth has gone through." A wise Greek had to listen to the judgment of a wise Egyptian. But nevertheless, the Greeks had not become so infantile as to demand of a growing youth, who was to be educated in one or another particular subject, that knowledge of the Egyptian language should first be acquired. They were very satisfied that the young person use the native Greek language. Unfortunately, we do not act today as the Greeks did, for we make our young people learn Greek. I do not want to speak against it; to learn Greek is something beautiful. But it is inconsistent with fulfilling the needs of a particular school age. It becomes a real problem when one is told to allocate so many lessons to this subject on the schedule at a time when such a claim clashes with the need for lessons in which weaving, spinning, and a rough knowledge of how paper is made should be practiced. Such is the situation when one is called on to finalize the schedule! And since we very well know that we shall never receive permission to build our own university anywhere, it is absolutely essential for us to enable those of our pupils who wish to continue their education at a university, technical college, or other similar institution, to pass the necessary graduation exam.

All this places us in an almost impossible situation, with almost insurmountable difficulties. When one tries to cultivate the practical side in education, prompted by insight into the inner needs of adolescent pupils, one has to face the bitter complaints of a Greek teacher who declares that the exam syllabus could never be covered with the amount of time allocated to the subject, and that, consequently, the candidates are doomed to fail their exams.

Such are the problems we have to tackle. They certainly show it is impossible for us to insist on pushing our ideals with any fanatical fervor. What will eventually have to happen no longer depends solely on the consensus of a circle of teachers about the rights and wrongs of education. Today it has become necessary for much wider circles within society to recognize the ideals of a truly human education, so that external conditions will render it possible for education to function without alienating pupils from life. This is obviously the case if, after having gone through a grammar school kind of education in one's own school, pupils were to fail their graduation exams, which they have to take somewhere else.[7]

---

7. Waldorf school pupils had to take the required graduation exams (*Abitur*) at a state school.

Speaking of failing an exam—and here I am speaking to specialists in education—I believe that it would be possible to make even a professor of botany, however clever, fail in botany—if that were the only intention! I really believe such a thing is possible, because anyone can fail an exam. In this chapter of life also, some very strange facts have shown up. There was, for example, Robert Hamerling, an Austrian poet, whose use of the German language was later acclaimed as the highest level any Austrian writer could possibly attain.[8] The results of his exam certificate, which qualified him for a teaching position at an Austrian *Gymnasium,* make interesting reading: Greek—excellent; Latin—excellent; German language and essay writing—hardly capable of teaching this subject in the lower classes of a middle school. You actually find this written in Hamerling's teaching certificate! So you see, this matter of failing or passing an exam is a very tricky business.

The difficulties that beset us, therefore, make us realize that society at large must provide better conditions before more can be accomplished than what is possible by making the kind of compromise I have spoken of. If I were to be asked, abstractly, whether a Waldorf school could be opened anywhere in the world, I could only answer, again entirely in the abstract, "Yes, wherever one would be allowed to open." On the other hand, even this would not be the determining factor because, as already said, in the eyes of many people these are only two aspects of one and the same thing. There are some who struggle through to become famous poets despite bad exam results in their main subject. But not everyone can do that. For many, a failed graduation exam means being cast out of the stream of life. And so it must be acknowledged that the higher the grade level in our school, the less one can work toward all of one's

8. Robert Hamerling (1830–1889) Austrian poet and philosopher.

educational ideals. It is something not to be forgotten. It shows how one has to come to terms with actual life situations.

The following question must always be present for an education based on an understanding of the human being: Will young people, as they enter life, find the proper human connection in society, which is a fundamental human need? After all, those responsible for the demands of graduation exams are also members of society, even if the style and content of their exams are based on error. Therefore, if one wants to integrate Waldorf pedagogy into present social conditions, one has to put up with having to do certain things that, in themselves, would not be considered right or beneficial. Anyone who inspects our top classes may well be under the impression that what is found there does not fully correspond to the avowed ideals of Waldorf pedagogy. But I can guarantee you that, if we were to carry out those ideals regardless of the general situation—and especially, if we attempted to make the transition to the practical side of life—all of our candidates for the graduation exam would fail! This is how diametrically opposed matters are today. But they have to be dealt with, and this can be done in great variety of ways. At the same time, awareness has to emerge regarding the degree of change necessary, not just in the field of education, but in all of life, before a truly human form of education can be established.

Despite all obstacles, the practical activities are being accomplished in the Waldorf school, at least to a certain extent—even though it does happen, now and then, that they have to be curtailed in some cases because the Greek or Latin teacher claims some of these lessons. That is something that cannot be avoided.

From what I've said, you can see that puberty is the proper time to make the transition, leading the adolescent into the realities of ordinary life. And the elements that will have to play more and more into school life, in a higher sense, are those that will make the human individual, as a being of body, soul, and spirit, a helpful and useful member of society. In this regard, our current time lacks the necessary psychological insight; for the finer interrelationships in the human spiritual, soul, and physical spheres are, in general, not even dreamed of. These things can be felt intuitively only by people who make it their particular task to come to understand the human psyche.

From personal self-knowledge I can tell you in all modesty that I could not have accomplished in spiritual science certain things that proved possible, if I had not learned bookbinding at a particular time in my life—which may seem somewhat useless to many people. And this was not in any way connected with Waldorf pedagogy, but simply a part of my destiny. This particularly human activity has particular consequences to most intimate spiritual and soul matters, especially if it is practiced at the right time of life. The same holds true for other practical activities as well. I would consider it a sin against human nature if we did not include bookbinding and box-making in our Waldorf school craft lessons, if it were not introduced into the curriculum at a particular age determined by insight into the students' development. These things are all part of becoming a full human being. The important thing in this case is not that a pupil makes a particular cardboard box or binds a book, but that the students have gone through the necessary discipline to make such items, and that they have experienced the inherent feelings and thought processes that go with them.

The natural differentiation between the boys and girls will become self-evident. Yet here one also needs to have an eye for what is happening, an eye of the soul. For example, the following situation has come up, the psychology of which has not yet been fully investigated, because I have not been able to spend enough time at the Waldorf school. We will investigate it thoroughly another time. But what happened was that, during lessons in spinning, the girls took to the actual spinning. The boys also wanted to be involved, and somehow they found their task in fetching and carrying for the girls. The boys wanted to be chivalrous. They brought the various materials that the girls then used for spinning. The boys seemed to prefer doing the preparatory work. This is what happened and we still need to digest it from the psychological perspective.

But this possibility of "switching our craft lessons around"— if I may put it that way—allows us to change to bookbinding now, and then to box-making. All are part of the practical activities that play a dominant role in Waldorf pedagogy, and they show how an eye for the practical side of life is a natural by-product for anyone who has made spiritual striving and spiritual research the main objective in life. There are educational methods in the world, the clever ideas of downright impractical theoreticians, who believe they have eaten practical life experience by the spoonful, methods that are nevertheless completely removed from reality. If one begins with theories of education, one will end up with the least practical results. Theories in themselves yield nothing useful, and too often breed only biases. A realistic pedagogy, on the other hand, is the offspring of true knowledge of the human being. And the part played by arts and crafts at a certain time of life is nothing but such knowledge applied to a particular situation. In itself this knowledge already presents a form of pedagogy that will turn into the right kind of practical teaching through the living way in which the actual lessons are given. It becomes transformed into the teacher's right attitude, and this is what really matters. The nature and character of the entire school has to be in tune with it.

And so, in the educational system cultivated in the Waldorf school, the center of gravity iis within the staff of teachers and their regular meetings, because the whole school is intended as one living and spirit-permeated organism. The first grade teacher is therefore expected to follow with real interest not only what the physics teacher is teaching to the seventh grade, but also the physics teacher's experiences of the various students in that class. This all flows together in the staff meetings, where practical advice and counseling, based on actual teaching experience, are freely given and received. Through the teaching staff a real attempt is made to create a kind of soul for the entire school organism. And so the first grade teacher will know that the sixth grade teacher has a child who is retarded in one way or another, or another who may be especially gifted. Such common interest and shared knowledge have a fructifying influence. The entire teaching body, being thus united, will experience the whole school as a unity. Then a common enthusiasm will pervade the school, but also a willingness to share in all its sorrows and worries. Then the entire teaching staff will carry whatever has to be carried, especially with regard to moral and religious issues, but also in matters of a more cognitive nature.

In this way, the different colleagues also learn how one particular subject, taught by one of the teachers, affects a completely different subject taught by another teacher. Just as, in the case of the human organism, it is not a matter of indifference whether the stomach is properly attuned to the head, so in a school it is not insignificant whether a lesson from nine to ten in the morning, given to the third grade, is properly related to the lesson from eleven to twelve in the eighth grade. This is in rather radical and extreme terms, of course. Things do not happen quite like that, but they are presented this way because they correspond essentially to reality. And if thinking is in touch with reality, judgments about matters pertaining to the sense-perceptible world will differ greatly from those based on abstract theories.

To illustrate this point I would like to mention certain lay healers who give medical treatment in places where this is not illegal. They are people who have acquired a certain measure of lay knowledge in medicine. Now one of these healers may find, for example, that a patient's heart is not functioning normally. This may be a correct diagnosis, but in this case it does not imply that the cure would be to bring the heart back to normality. And according to such a lay healer, the patient may have adapted the entire organism to the slightly abnormal function of the heart. This means that if now one were to get the heart to work normally again, such a "cured" heart, just because of its return to normality, might upset the entire organism, thus causing a deterioration of the patient's general condition. Consequently the therapy could actually consist of leaving the heart as it is, with the recommendation that, should the symptoms of the slight heart defect return, a different course of treatment should be given from what would normally be done through the use of medications under similar circumstances.

I said yesterday that educating and healing are related activities. And so something similar is also called for in the field of education. That is, a kind of conceptual and sensitive feeling approach, both comprehensive and in touch with reality, since it would have to apply to other realms of cognition directly related to practical life.

If we look at what contemporary anatomy and physiology tell us about the human being—not to mention psychology, which is a hodgepodge of abstractions anyway—we find a certain type of knowledge from which a picture of the human being is manufactured. If this picture is used as a means of self-knowledge, it creates the impression that we are merely a skeleton. (Within certain limits, knowledge of the human being is also self-knowledge—not the introspective kind, but rather a recognition of essentially human qualities found in each individual.) If, when looking at ourselves, we had to disregard. everything within and around our skeleton, we would naturally conclude that we were only skeletons. This is how the whole human being—body, soul, and spirit—would appear to us if we used only what contemporary anatomy and physiology offers as a picture of the human being. Psychology needs to truly permeate the human psyche with spirit. If this is done, we can follow the spiritual element right into the physical realities of the body, because spirit works in every part of the human body.

I have already said that the tragedy of materialism is its inability to understand the true nature of matter. Knowledge of spirit leads to true understanding of matter. Materialism may speak of matter, but it does not penetrate to the inner structures of the forces that work through matter. Similarly, pedagogy that observes only external phenomena does not penetrate to the regions of the human being that reveal what should be done about practical life. This causes a situation that, to the spiritual investigator, is very natural, but would appear paradoxical for many people. They wonder why a pedagogy grown from anthroposophy always emphasizes the necessity of training children at specific ages in certain practical activities—that is, the necessity of training them in the correct handling of material processes. Far from leading students into a foggy mysticism, the principles and methods of the education based on anthroposophical research will not estrange them from life. On the contrary, it will induce spirit and soul substance to penetrate their physical bodies, thus making them useful for this earthly life, and at the same time, provide them with the proper conditions to develop inner certainty. This is why we feel it necessary to expand the practical type of work, and, of course, difficulties therefore increase with the beginning of every new school year when we have to add a new class to the existing ones (we began with eight grades, adding the ninth, tenth, and eleventh, and we are about to open our first twelfth grade).

This has led to the situation where, while other problems facing the anthroposophical cause were being dealt with very recently, a memorandum was handed in by the pupils of the current highest grade level in the Waldorf school. Those among them who were expecting to have to take their graduation exam had worked out a remarkable document, the deeper aspects of which will be appreciated only when the whole matter is seen in the proper light. They had sent more or less the following memorandum to the Anthroposophical Society:

> Since we are being educated and taught in the sense of the true human being [they had somehow gleaned this] and, consequently, since we cannot enter existing types of colleges, we wish to make the following proposal to the Anthroposophical Society: That a new anthroposophical college is to be founded where we can continue our education.

No negative judgment regarding colleges in general is implied in this wording, although such judgments are frequently encountered in contemporary society.

All of this presents us with the greatest difficulties. But since you have made the effort to come here to find out what Waldorf pedagogy is all about—something we very well know how to appreciate—these problems should also be aired. Any sincere interest in what is willed in this education deserves a clear indication of all the difficulties involved.

Thus far, Waldorf pedagogy is being practiced only by the teachers of the one existing Waldorf school, and there we find our difficulties increase the higher we go with the school. I can only assume that the problems would be even greater in a college operated anthroposophically. But since such a college is only a very abstract ideal, I can only speak about it hypothetically. It has always been my way to deal directly with the tasks set by life, and this is why I can talk about this education only up to the twelfth grade, which is opening soon. Things that belong to a misty future must not take up too much time for people standing amid life, since it would only detract from the actual tasks at hand.

One can say only that problems would increase substantially, and that obviously there would be two kinds of difficulties. First, if we were to open a college, our exam results would not be recognized as proper qualifications, which means that successful candidates could not take up professional positions in life. They could not become medical doctors, lawyers, and so on; professions that in their present customary forms are still essential today. This presents one side of the problem. The other side would conjure up really frightening prospects, if certain hard facts did not offer relief from such anxieties; for, on the strength of the praiseworthy efforts made by our young friends, an association has actually been founded with the express aim of working toward the creation of such a college, based on the principles of Waldorf pedagogy. The only reason there is no need to feel thoroughly alarmed about the potential consequences of such an endeavor is that the funds needed by this association will certainly not reach such giddy heights that anyone would be tempted to seriously consider going ahead with the project. The underlying striving toward this aim is thoroughly laudable, but for the time being it remains beyond the realm of practicality. The real worry would come only if, for example, an American millionaire were to suddenly offer the many millions needed to build, equip, and staff such a college. The best one could do in such a situation would be to promote, en masse, the entire teaching staff of the Waldorf school to become the teachers of the new college. But then there would no longer be a Waldorf school!

I am saying all this because I believe actual facts are far more important than any kind of abstract argument. While acknowledging that the idea of basing education, including college education, on true knowledge of the human being represents a far-reaching ideal, we must not overlook the fact that the circle of those who stand firmly behind our ideals is extremely small. This is the very reason one feels so happy about every move toward an expansion of this work, which may gain further momentum through your welcome visit to this course. At the same time, one must never lose sight of all that must happen so that the Waldorf ideal can rest upon truly firm and sound foundations. This needs to be mentioned within the context of this course, for it follows from the constitution of the Waldorf school.

Tomorrow, in the concluding lecture, I would like to tell you more about this constitution of the Waldorf school—about how it is run, about what the relationship should be between teachers and students, as well as the interrelationships of pupils among themselves, and teachers among themselves. Furthermore, I would like to speak about what, in our way of thinking, are the proper methods of dealing with exams and school reports, so that they reflect knowledge of the human being.

Lecture Eight

In order to round off, so to speak, what we could only superficially outline during the last few days regarding education based
on anthroposophical investigations, I would like to add something today, as an example of how these ideas can be put into
practice, about how the Waldorf school is run. What has to
emerge clearly from the spirit of this education is that equal consideration be given to everything pertaining to the human body,
soul, and spirit. If the actual teaching is carried out as characterized, therefore, it will at the same time become a kind of hygiene
in the life of the child and, if necessary, even a therapy.

To see this clearly, one has to be able to look at the child's
being in the right way. And here it must be understood that
everything we have said about the child's development, from
birth to the change of teeth, is revealed most of all in the activities of the nerve-sense system. Every organic system naturally
extends over the entire human body, but each system is at the
same time localized in a definite part of the physical organism.
Thus the nervous system is mainly organized in the head. But
when speaking about the three main organic systems of the
human being—the *nerve-sense system, the rhythmic system,* and
the metabolic-motor system—we do not imply that they are

confined only to the head, the chest, and the metabolic-limb systems, because this would be completely inaccurate. It is impossible to divide the human organization into three separate spatial regions. It can only be said that these three systems interpenetrate one another, that they work and weave into each other everywhere.

The nerve-sense system is, nevertheless, localized primarily in the region of the head. The rhythmic system, which includes everything of a rhythmic nature in the human being, is mainly organized in the chest organs, in the organs of breathing and blood circulation. Here one must not ignore the fact that everything that furthers the rhythms of digestion—and ultimately those of sleeping and waking—also belongs to the rhythmic system, insofar as digesting, and sleeping and waking are based physically within the human organism. The actual chemical-physiological process of digestion is closely connected with all that forms the human motor system. As for movement itself, a reciprocal activity occurs between the nutritional and digestive system on the one hand, and the actual physical movement on the other.

All of this means that, although the three systems work naturally into each other during the child's early years until the change of teeth, the formative and malleable shaping forces involved in the child's growth and nourishing processes work mainly downward from the head, the center of the senses and the nervous system. Consequently, if a young child becomes ill, that illness is due primarily to the influences of the nerve-sense system. That is why young children before their second dentition are especially likely to suffer from illnesses that originate from within—those called childhood illnesses.

The influences that emanate from the environment, those that reach children through their urge to imitate, have a very powerful effect on this vulnerability to childhood illnesses, more than is commonly realized by the medical profession within the current materialistic climate. Thus, a sudden outburst of anger by an adult, when witnessed by a young child, can be responsible in many cases for an attack of measles. I am not referring to the psychopathic outburst of a psychopath, but to a less violent form of temper that can very often be seen among people. The shock that follows, together with its moral and spiritual implications, must certainly be seen as a contributing factor for measles. Furthermore, all these influences that work on the child will remain as after-effects until almost the ninth year. If a teacher happens to become very angry in school (for example, if a child accidentally spills some ink, and the teacher reacts by shouting, "If you do that again, I'll pour the entire inkwell over your head!" or "I'll throw it at your head!"), then we shouldn't be surprised when this has a very damaging effect on the child's physical health. Of course, I have chosen a fairly drastic example, but this kind of thing can happen too easily in a classroom.

Inner dishonesty in teachers also has a very harmful effect on children, even after their second dentition. Falsehoods can take on many different guises, such as insincerity or hypocritical piety, or establishing a moral code for the children that the adults would not dream of applying to themselves. In such cases the element of untruth weaves and lives in the words spoken, and in what unfolds in front of the child. An adult may remain totally oblivious to it, but children will take it in through the teachers' gestures. Through the nerve-sense system, dishonesty and hypocrisy have an extremely powerful effect on the organic structure of the child's digestive tract, and especially on the development of the gall bladder, which can then play a very significant role for the rest of the child's life.

All pedagogical interactions have to be permeated by this intensive awareness of how spirit, soul, and body constantly interweave and affect each other, even though it is unnecessary for teachers to speak of it all the time. And since the human organism, from the head downward, is so active during these early years—that is, from the polarity of the nerve-sense system—and because abnormal conditions can easily override so-called normal conditions in the head region, the child is particularly vulnerable to childhood diseases at just this age.

The years between the change of teeth and puberty, strangely enough (and yet, true to the nature of the human organism) are the child's healthiest years, although this is not really surprising to anyone with insight into human development. This is because the child's entire organic structure at this age radiates from the rhythmic system. This is the very system that never becomes tired or overstimulated on its own. Symptoms of illness that occur during these years are due to outer circumstances, although this statement must not be taken too strictly, of course, and only within the context of actual life situations. The child who is subject to illness at this particular age, when the rhythmic system plays such a dominant part has been treated improperly, one way or another, in outer life.

When puberty is left behind, the occurrence of illness radiates outward from within—that is, from the metabolic-motor system. That is the time of life when the causes of illness, to which young people are exposed, arise from within. Because the method of teaching the actual lessons plays a large part in the physical well-being of the students, we must always allow a certain physical and soul hygiene to be carried, as if on wings, by our educational ideas and methods. This must always be part of whatever we do with our classes, particularly during the second period of childhood.

Here certain details can be indicated. Let us take, for example, a child with a melancholic disposition. If you give that child sugar—an appropriate amount, of course—you will find that the sugar has a totally different effect than it would have on a predominantly sanguine child. In a melancholic child the sugar will have a suppressive effect on liver activity. This gradual lessening of liver activity, in radiating out into the entire being of the child, effectively curbs the melancholic tendencies from the physical side. It is a useful expedient, but one has to understand it. Using it as an aid does not mean the denial of soul and spirit, because anyone who knows that spirit is working in all physical or material processes—as anthroposophy reveals—will not view the effect of an increased sugar-intake on the activity of the liver as something merely physical, but as the working of soul and spirit brought about by physical means. (Naturally, the result always depends on the correct dosage.) In the case of a sanguine child it can be beneficial to stimulate liver activity by withholding sugar.

This is an example of how knowledge of the interaction and mutual working of body, soul, and spirit can greatly benefit the three systems of the human being. It definitely allows one to say as well that, contrary to frequently held opinions, Waldorf pedagogy (which arises from spiritual foundations) certainly does not neglect the physical aspects of education. On the other hand, you will find that other forms of pedagogy, bent on developing the physical part of the child according to fixed, abstract rules indeed serve it least, because their adherents do not realize that every soul and spiritual stirring within a child has a direct effect on his or her physical nature.

Because of all this, I felt it necessary to give a seminar course before the opening of the Waldorf school, for the benefit of those who had been chosen to become its first teachers.[1] One

---

1. See Rudolf Steiner, *The Foundations of Human Experience*, Anthroposophic Press, Hudson, NY, 1996, and *Practical Advice to Teachers*, Rudolf Steiner Press, London, 1976, and *Discussions with Teachers*, Rudolf Steiner Press, London, 1967.

of the primary aims of this course was to bring the fundamental and comprehensive thought of the working together of soul, body, and spirit into the new pedagogy before its actual launching; for knowledge of this has been lost gradually during the nineteenth and twentieth centuries—more so than is generally realized.

During the years after the Waldorf school founding, shorter supplementary courses were also given.[2] It goes without saying that anyone who seriously considers taking an active role in Waldorf education must live in the spirit of these courses. This is what really matters. If one wants to treat a certain subject in a living way, the details are not as important, because they can always be worked out of the spiritual background. The details will then also appear in proper perspective. You may already have seen, through talks given by Waldorf teachers such as Dr. von Baravalle[3] and Dr. von Heydebrand,[4] how the attempt was made to let the spirit living in this education flow into the ways of teaching various subjects. Something like lifeblood will pulse through the lessons when the human structure is comprehended in terms of an all-comprising spiritual entity. In this respect, of course, much of what can be said today will have to remain brief and superficial.

I mentioned yesterday that a united faculty of teachers, functioning like the soul and spirit of the entire school organism, is absolutely fundamental to running a Waldorf school. According to one of its pedagogical impulses, it is not so much a statistical collection of the teachers' observations expressed during

2. See *Balance in Teaching*, Mercury Press, Spring Valley, NY, 1990; *Education for Adolescents*, Anthroposophic Press, Hudson, NY, 1996; and *Deeper Insights into Education* (to be republished).
3. Dr. Herman von Baravalle (1898–1973) teacher of mathematics and physics at the Waldorf school in Stuttgart.
4. Caroline von Heydebrand (1866–1938) class teacher at the Waldorf school.

the meetings that is important, but that a living and individu-alizing psychology should be jointly developed from out of the actual experience of teaching lessons. I would like to give you an example.

In our school, boys and girls sit next to each other. When we started, there were just over one hundred students in the Wal-dorf school. But our numbers have grown so quickly that we had seven hundred pupils last year, which necessitated opening paral-lel classes, especially in the lower grades of the school. Now we find that there are more girls than boys in some classes, while in others there are more boys. The number of boys and girls more or less even in very few classes. To insist on equal numbers in each class would not only be pedantic, but would not work. First of all, new arrivals do not come neatly paired, and, second, such a scheme would not represent real life. The right way to proceed in such a situation is to make it possible to apply educational impulses whatever the outer circumstances may be.

All the same, we soon found that a class with a majority of girls presented a very different psychological picture than those with more boys, aside from outer circumstances—that is, aside from the most obvious. What gives such a class its psychologi-cal character is the imponderable element that easily escapes one's notice. Nevertheless, when working together in our meet-ings, the opportunity was presented to make fruitful investiga-tions in this direction. And it soon became clear that sharing such questions of common interest greatly contributed to the school's becoming a living, ensouled organism.

Let's imagine someone who says, "I want to think only thoughts that will be useful to me later in life. I don't want to allow anything to enter my soul that does not have direct value for later life, because this would be uneconomical." Such a per-son would become an appalling figure in life! First, because such a person would have nothing to dream about—indeed, could never dream. Of course, people who are inclined in this direction might simply reply, "Dreams are unimportant. One can very well do without them, because they really don't mean anything in life." True, dreams have little consequence for those who accept only external reality. But what if there were more to dreams than just fantastic images? Naturally, those who believe they see something highly significant and deeply prophetic in every dream, even if it is only caused by the activities of their liver, bladder, or stomach—people who consider dreams more important than events in waking life—they will not draw any benefit from their dreaming. Yet, if one knows that in one's dream life forces are expressed—even if only indistinctly—that have either a health-giving or an illness-inducing effect on the breathing, circulatory, and nerve-sense systems, then one also knows that half of the human being is mirrored in these dreams, either in a hygienic or in a pathological sense. Further, one will recognize that not to dream at all would be similar to undermining the digestion or circulation through taking some form of poison. It is important to realize that much of what may appear unnecessary in a human being for outer life, nevertheless, plays an important part—similar to the way we see outer nature. Just compare the infinite number of herring eggs, distributed all over the seas, with the number of herrings actually born, and you could easily reproach nature for being tremendously wasteful. However, this could only be the opinion of those who do not know of the powerful spiritual effects the dead herring eggs have on the growing herrings. A certain number of eggs have to die so that a certain number of eggs may thrive. These things are all interconnected.

If we now relate this thought to the school as a living organism, we have the following situation: In the staff meetings of our teachers such matters as the proportion of boys to girls, and many other problems, are being worked through from a psychological and pneumatological aspect as part of a common study of soul and spirit. Efforts are made continually to effect a new understanding of the psychological and pathological problems facing the school. And, in order to cover every contingency, something else is essential in the life of a school, something we have in the Waldorf school, and that is a school doctor. He is a full-time staff member, who also teaches various classes in the school. This allows the teachers—insofar as they actively take part in all the meetings—to discuss and work through pathological and therapeutic questions, as well as those posed by the specially gifted child. Problems are studied not only for the benefit of individual cases—more or less statistically—but they are worked through in depth. In this way, much can be learned from each individual case, even if it does not always appear to be immediately useful.

One could compare this situation with someone who has taken in one thing or another, and declares it to be of no use in life. Nevertheless, life may prove otherwise. Similarly, whatever is worked through by the teachers in these meetings, creating a living psychology, a living physiology, and so on, continues to have an effect, often in very unexpected places. Imagine you had occupied yourself, let's say, with the spiritual functions of a child's gall—forgive this expression, but it is fully justified— and that through this study you had learned to find a way into this kind of thinking. If you were now suddenly called on to deal with a child's nose, you actually would relate very differently to the new situation. Even if you may think, "What is the good of learning all about the gall if now I have to deal with the nose?" Once you find a point of entry, you meet every problem and task differently.

In this sense, the teaching faculty must become the spirit and soul of the entire school organism. Only then will each teacher enter the classroom with the proper attitude and in the right soul condition. At the same time, we must also remember that, in just these matters, an intensely religious element can be found. It is unnecessary to have the name of the Lord constantly on one's lips or to call on the name of Christ all the time. It is better to adhere to the command: "Thou shalt not take the name of the Lord God in vain." Nevertheless, it is possible to permeate one's entire life with a fundamental religious impulse, with an intensely Christian impulse. Certain experiences of old, no longer known to the modern mind, will then begin to stir in one's soul, experiences deeply rooted in human evolution, in the Christian development of humankind. For example, teachers who in the depths of their souls are seeking the proper stimulation for finding appropriate forms of pedagogy (especially in these pathological-physiological areas) would do well to allow themselves to be inspired, time and again, by what radiates from the Gospel of Saint Luke. (To modern ears such a statement must sound bizarre.) On the other hand, teachers who want to instill the necessary idealism for life in their students, would do well to find a source of inspiration by reading again and again the Gospel of Saint John. If teachers do not want their pupils to grow up into cowards, but into the kind of people who will tackle life's tasks with exuberant energy, they should look for inspiration in the Gospel of Saint Mark. And those who are enthusiastic to educate the young to grow into perceptive adults, rather than into people who go through life with unseeing eyes, may find the necessary stimulation in the Gospel of Saint Matthew. These are the qualities that, in ancient times, were felt to live in the different Gospels. If our contemporaries were to read that in past ages the Gospel of Saint Luke was felt to radiate a healing element in a medical sense, they could not make anything of it. On the other hand, if they entered life as real pedagogues, they would begin to understand such matters again.

This is one way one can speak about these things. It is just as possible to speak of them in an entirely different way, no less religious or Christian. For instance, the main theme during a seminar course could well be the four temperaments of the human being—that is, the psychic, physical, and spiritual natures of the choleric, melancholic, sanguine, and phlegmatic temperaments. First, one would give a description of these four temperaments and then one could discuss how they must be treated in class. For example, it has a salutary effect if one seats choleric children together in one corner of the classroom, giving a certain relief in this way to the rest of the class, because the teacher is freed from having to constantly discipline them. Choleric children can't help pushing and hitting each other. If they now find themselves suddenly at the receiving end, this in itself produces a thoroughly pedagogical effect, because the ones who do the pushing and shoving, goading others into retaliating, are being "shaped up" in a very direct way. And if, by seating the phlegmatics together, one lets them "phlegmatize" each other, this also has a wonderfully pedagogical effect. However, all this needs to be done with the appropriate tact. One really has to know how to handle the situation in each individual case. You will find a detailed treatment of the children's various temperaments in the published version of the first training course, given to the teachers of the Waldorf school.[5]

What I have said about the four Gospels, fundamentally speaking, is exactly the same when seen from a spiritual perspective, because it leads one into the same element of life. Today it is ordinarily felt that, if one wants to learn something, the relevant elements have to be put neatly side by side. But

---

5. See footnote page 171. See also the 1909 lecture, "The Four Temperaments," contained in Rudolf Steiner, *Anthroposophy in Everyday Life*, Anthroposophic Press, Hudson, NY, 1995.

this is a procedure that will not lead to fundamental principles, as they have to be dealt with in actual life. For example, one cannot understand the human gall or liver system unless one also has an understanding of the human head, because every organ in the digestive tract has a complementary organ in the brain. One does not know anything about the liver unless one also knows its correlative function in the brain. Likewise, one does not have an inner understanding of the immense inspiration that can flow into the human soul from the Gospels, unless one can also transform these into the ways that character and temperament are imprinted into the human individuality here on Earth. To livingly comprehend the world is very different from comprehending it through dead concepts.

This will also help one to see that if children are raised in light of the education spoken of here, one allows something to grow in them that will outlast their childhood days, something that will continue to affect them throughout their lives; for what do you have to do when you grow old? People who do not understand human nature cannot assess how important certain impulses, which can be implanted only during childhood, are for life. At that tender age it is still possible for these impulses to be immersed into the soft and pliable organism of the child, still very open to the musical-formative forces. In later years the organism becomes harder, not necessarily physically, but in any case, tending toward psycho-bodily hardening. What one has absorbed through one's upbringing and education, however, does not grow old. No matter how old one has become, one is still inwardly endowed with the same youthful element that one had from, say, the tenth to the fifteenth year. One always carries this element of youthfulness within, but it has to remain supple and flexible to the degree that the now aged brain—perhaps already covered by a bald head—can use it in the same way that the previously soft brain did. If a person's education has not helped this process, however, the result is a generation gap, which appears so often these days, and is considered unbridgeable.

Sometimes people say something that is actually the opposite of what is really happening. For example, one often hears the comment, "The young today don't understand the elderly, because old people no longer know how to be young with the young." But this is not the truth. Not at all. What really happens is that the young generation expects the old generation to be able to properly use the physical organization which has grown old. In this way, young people recognize something in the old that is different from their own condition, something they do not yet have. This is the quality that leads to the natural respect for old age. When young people meet an old person who can still use an already-bald head in the way children use their tousled heads, they feel that something can be received from the older generation, something that they cannot find in their contemporaries. This is how it should be.

We must educate young people so that they know how to grow old properly. It is the malaise of our time that as young people grow up, they do not recognize among the older generation those who have aged properly. They see merely childish individuals, instead, who have remained at the same level of development as the young generation. This is because of the inadequate education of old people who cannot properly use their physical organization, and they remain infantile. The expression "overgrown kids" is really chosen with great ingenuity, for it implies that such persons lost the ability to get hold of their entire organism during the course of their lives.[6] They can work only with the head, which is precisely what children or young people are meant to do. So the young

---

6. The German expression is *Kindskopf,* literally "child's head." — TRANS.

respond by saying, "Why should we learn from them? They are no further along than we are; they are just as childish as we are." The point is not that old age lacks youthfulness, but that it has remained behind, is too infantile, and this causes difficulties today. You see how expressions, sometimes chosen with the most goodwill, mean the opposite of what they intend convey.[7]

These things must all be seen in the proper light before education can stand on its feet again. This has become more than necessary today. Forgive this somewhat drastic way of saying it, but in our intellectual age education really has been turned upside-down.

Thus, one of the characteristic features of Waldorf pedagogy is to learn that it is not the externals that are important. Whether a teacher draws substance to nourish the souls of students from the different qualities of the four Gospels, or whether this is done by using what was presented in the Stuttgart teachers' training course with regard to the four temperaments does not matter at all. What does matter is the spirit that reigns in everything developed there. Because of how superficially these things are often regarded today, it could

---

7. See Rudolf Steiner's *The Youth Section of the School of Spiritual Science,* March 9, 1924 (published in *The Constitution of the School of Spiritual Science,* Anthroposophical Society in Great Britain, 1964), which states:

But the youth today does not see in the older men and women any human quality different from its own, yet worthy of its emulation. For the older people of the present day are not really "old." They have taken in the content of many things and can talk of these. But their knowledge has not ripened in them. They have grown older in years, but in the soul they have not kept pace with the advancing years. They speak out of an older brain in just the same way that they spoke when the brain was young. Young people feel this fact. They do not perceive maturity when they are with their elders; they see their own young condition of soul in older bodies, and they turn away, for this does not seem true to them.

easily happen that someone, when told that the treatment of the four temperaments could be studied in the fundamental course given in Stuttgart, could also consult a later course where one would find something about the teacher's attitude toward the four Gospels. The reaction of such a person might well be, "In this case, I should study the later course as well." It certainly is a good thing to approach different subjects by using different sources. But there is also another way of looking at it—that is, one may find a common message running through both courses, given in two different places at different times, even though outwardly the subjects may appear very different. This inner correspondence found within different lecture courses can be uncomfortable because of the way their various points are interlinked, instead of fitting into the more conventional patterns of cause and effect.

Thus, the educational course given here at the Goetheanum just over a year ago (where some English friends were present, and which was rendered very competently and artistically by Mister Steffen[8]) can be compared with what I presented to you again differently in this course.[9] You will find that, basically, the substance of both courses is the same as, for example, the head and the stomach; each form a part of one organism. It may be uncomfortable that, because of how various themes mutually support each other, one cannot say: I have read and understood the first course; and because the later one is supposed to carry the same message, there is no need for me to study it as well. The fact is, however, that, if one has studied both courses, the earlier one will be understood in greater

---

8. Albert Steffen (1884–1963), Swiss poet, novelist, playwright, and a leading student of Rudolf Steiner beginning in 1907.
9. See Rudolf Steiner, *Soul Economy and Waldorf Education,* Anthroposophic Press, Hudson, NY, 1986.

depth, because each sheds light on the other. It could even be said that, only when one has digested a later teachers' course, can one fully understand an earlier one because of these reciprocal effects. Mathematics is built on purely causal sequences, so it is possible to understand earlier stages without any knowledge of subsequent stages. But when it comes to teaching in a living way, its subject is affected by mutual interconnections, so that what was given at an earlier date may receive further elucidation by what was presented later.

I mention this because it is all part of the living spirit that has to permeate the Waldorf way of teaching. One has to have the good will that wants to know it from all sides, and one must never be satisfied with having comprehended one particular aspect of it. As a Waldorf teacher, one has to be conscious of the necessity for continually widening and deepening one's knowledge, rather than feeling satisfied with one's achievements and, indeed, considering oneself very clever. If one has lived into the Waldorf way of teaching, such delusions are soon overcome! For a real Waldorf teacher, everything that flows from this activity must be permeated with true heart and soul forces. It has to spring from the right kind of self-confidence, which rests on trust in God. When there is awareness of the divine forces working within, one will be fed by a constantly flowing fountain of life, flowing since time beyond memory, and very much apart from what one may or may not have learned externally. It is only the beginning of the way when self-confidence stems from outer achievements. One is in the proper place when self-confidence has led to confidence in the working of God, when it has led to an awareness of the power of the words: *Not I, but the Christ in me.* When this happens, self-confidence also becomes self-modesty, because one realizes that the divine forces of Christ are reflected in whatever is carried in one's soul. This spirit must reign throughout the school.

If it were not present, the school would be like a natural organism whose lifeblood was being drawn out, or that was slowly being asphyxiated.

This is the spirit that is most important, and if it is alive, it will engender enthusiasm, regardless of the staff or the leadership of the school. One can then be confident that a somewhat objective spirit will live throughout the school, which is not the same as the sum of the teachers' individual spirits. This, however, can be nurtured only gradually within the life of the teaching staff.

As a result of working in this way, something has emerged in the Waldorf school that we call "block periods" or "main lessons." These main lessons—much longer than the ordinary lessons, which allow one subject to be studied in depth—do not distract children, as often happens because of too many subject changes. For example, students might typically be given a geography lesson from 8 to 8:45 A.M., followed by an entirely different subject, such as Latin, from 8:45 until 9:30 A.M. This might be followed again by math, or some other lesson. Block periods of main lessons, on the other hand, are structured so that the same subject is taught every day for about three or four weeks (depending on the type of subject) during the first half of the morning session. For example, in a main lesson period, geography would be studied for perhaps three or four weeks— not severely or in a heavy-handed way, but in a more relaxed, yet completely serious way. When the same subject is taken up again during one of the following terms, it will build on what was given during the previous block period. In this way, the subject matter covered during one year is taught in block periods instead of during regular weekly lessons. This method is, no doubt, more taxing for teachers than the conventional schedule arrangements would be, because such lengthy geography lessons could easily become boring for the children. This is solved by the teachers' much deeper immersion in the subjects, so that they are equal to their freely-chosen tasks.

After a mid-morning break, which is essential for the children, the main lesson is usually followed by language lessons, or by other subjects not taught in main lesson periods. Two foreign languages are introduced to our pupils as soon as they enter the first grade in a Waldorf school. Using our own methods, we teach them French and English—the aim not being so much a widening of their outer horizons, but an enrichment of their soul life.

You will ascertain from what was said yesterday that physical movement, practiced most of all in eurythmy and gymnastics, is by no means considered to be less important, but is dealt with so that it can play a proper role within the total curriculum. Similarly, right from the beginning in the first grade, all lessons are permeated by a musical element according to various ages and stages.

I have already indicated (with unavoidable briefness, unfortunately) how our pupils are being directed into artistic activities—into singing, music-making, modeling, and so on. It is absolutely necessary to nurture these activities. Simply through practicing them with the children, one will come to realize exactly what it means for their entire lives to be properly guided musically during these younger years, from the change of teeth through the ninth and twelfth years until puberty. Proper introduction to the musical element is fundamental for a human being to overcome any hindrance that impedes, later in life, a sound development of a will permeated with courage. Musical forces effect the human organism by allowing, as smoothly as possible, the nerve fluctuations to become active in the stream of breath. The breath-stream, in turn, works back upon the functions of the nervous system. The breathing rhythms then work over into the rhythms of the blood circulation, which in turn act on the rhythms of sleeping and waking. This insight, afforded by anthroposophical investigation, of how musical forces creatively work within the structure of the human being, is one of the most wonderful things in life.

One learns to recognize that we have an extremely sensitive and refined musical instrument in the raying out of the nerves from the spinal marrow, from the entire system of the spinal cord. One also learns to see how this delicate instrument dries up and hardens, whereby, inwardly, the human being can no longer properly develop qualities of courage, if musical instruction and the general musical education do not work harmoniously with this wonderfully fine musical instrument. What constitutes a truly delicate and unique musical instrument is coming into being through the mutual interplay between the organs of the nerves and senses with their functions on the one hand, and on the other hand, the human motor functions with their close affinities to the digestive rhythms and those of sleeping and waking.

The upper part of the human being wants to influence the lower part. By directing the child's entire organism toward the realm of music, we enhance the merging of external sounds (from a piano during music lessons, or from the children's singing voices) with the nervous and circulatory systems, in what can be recognized as a divine plan of creation. This is a sublime thing, because in every music lesson there is a meeting between the divine-spiritual and what comes from the earthly realm, rising, as it were, within the child's body. Heaven and Earth truly meet in every achievement of musical culture throughout human earthly evolution, and we should always be aware of this. This awareness, plus the teachers' knowledge that they are instrumental in bringing together the genius of Heaven with the genius of Earth, gives them the enthusiasm they need to face their classes. This same enthusiasm is also carried into the teachers' staff meetings where the music teacher may inspire the art teacher, and so on. Here you can see clearly how essential it is that spirit works through every aspect of Waldorf education.

To give another example: not long ago, during one of our teacher meetings, it truly became possible to work out to a large extent what happens to the students' spirit, soul, and body, when first given eurythmy exercises and then directed in doing gymnastics. Such insight into the relationship between gymnastics and eurythmy (which is very important to how these lessons are presented) was really accomplished in one of our teacher meetings the other day. Of course, we will continue our research. But, this is how teacher meetings become like the blood that must flow through the school as a living organism. Everything else will fall into place, as long as that is allowed to happen.

Teachers will know also when it is proper to take their classes for a walk or for an outing, and the role of gymnastics will find a natural and appropriate place within the life of the students, regardless of which school they attend. Doubts and anxieties will disappear with regard to the remark: What is done in a Waldorf school may all be very good, but they neglect sports there. Admittedly, it is not yet possible for us to do everything that may be desirable, because the Waldorf school has had to develop from small beginnings. Only by overcoming enormous obstacles and external difficulties was it possible to have gone as far as we have today. But when matters are taken care of with spiritual insight, the whole question of the relationship between physical and spiritual will be handled properly.

The following analogy could be used: Just as it is unnecessary to learn how the various larger and smaller muscles of the arm function (according to the laws of dynamics and statics, of vitalism, and so on) so that one can lift it, so it is also unnecessary to know every detail of the ins-and-outs of everything that must be done, as long as we can approach and present lessons out of the spirit that has become transformed into the proper attitude of the teacher—as long as we can penetrate properly to the very essence of all our tasks and duties.

I could only give you brief and superficial outlines of the fundamental principles and impulses, flowing from anthroposophical research, according to which the Waldorf school functions. And so we have come to the end of this course—primarily because of your other commitments.

At this point I would like to express once more what I already said during one of our discussions: If one lives with heart and soul, with the ideal of allowing education to grow into a blessing for all humankind in its evolution, one is filled with deep gratitude when meeting teachers from so many different places; for you have come to this course to obtain information about the way of teaching that arises from anthroposophical investigation, which I have attempted to place before you. Beyond whether this was received by one or another participant with more or less sympathy, I want to express my deep gratitude and inner satisfaction that it was again possible for a large group of souls to perceive what is intended to work on the most varied branches of life, and what is meant to fructify life in general through anthroposophy. Two thoughts will remain with you, especially with those who dealt with the organization and practical arrangements of this course: the happy memory of the gratitude, and the happy memory of the inner satisfaction as I expressed it just now. And the more intensely these thoughts can be inwardly formed—the thoughts of the work based on such gratitude and satisfaction—the more hope will grow that, in times to come, this way of teaching may yet succeed for the benefit of all of humanity.

Such hope will intensify the loving care for this way of teaching in those who already have the will to devote themselves to it with all their human qualities.

It should also be said that it was not only the Waldorf teachers who may have given you something of their practical experience, because those of you who have been present here as visitors have certainly given equally to them. By allowing us to witness what lives in us begin to live in other souls as well, you have fanned the glow of love that is both necessary and natural, and just that can engender genuine enthusiasm. And we may hope that out of feelings of gratitude and inner satisfaction, of hope and love that have flowed together during this course, good fruits may ripen, provided we can maintain the necessary interest in these matters, and that we are inwardly active enough to sustain them.

Ladies and gentlemen, my dear friends, this is what I want to pour into my farewell, which is not to be taken as formal or abstract, but as very concrete, in which gratitude becomes a firm foundation, and inner satisfaction a source of warmth, from which hope will radiate out, bringing both courage and strength. May the love of putting into practice what is willed to become a way of teaching for all human beings be turned into light that shines for those who feel it their duty to care for the education of all humankind!

In this sense, having to bring this course to its conclusion, I wish to give you all my warmest farewell greetings.

Question: Would it be possible to implement the Waldorf way of teaching in other countries, in Czechoslovakia, for example?

RUDOLF STEINER: In principle it is possible to introduce Waldorf education anywhere, because it is based purely on pedagogy. This is the significant difference between Waldorf pedagogy and other educational movements. As you know, there are people today who maintain that if one wants to give pupils a proper education, one must send them to a country school, because they consider an urban environment unsuitable for children's education. Then there are those who hold the opinion that only a boarding school can offer the proper conditions for their children's education, while still others insist that only life at home can provide the proper background for children. All of these things cease to be of real importance in Waldorf education. I do not wish to quarrel about these different attitudes (each of which may have its justification from one or another point of view), but since Waldorf education focuses entirely on the pedagogical aspect, it can be adapted to any outer conditions, whether a city school, a country school or whatever. It is not designed to meet specific external conditions, but is based entirely on observation and insight into the growing human being. This means that Waldorf pedagogy could be implemented in every school.

Whether this would be allowed to happen, whether the authorities that oversee education, the establishing of curricula, and so on would ever agree to such a step being taken, is an entirely different question. There is nothing to stop Waldorf pedagogy from being applied anywhere in the world, even tomorrow, but the real question is whether permission for this to happen would be granted. This question can be answered only in terms of the various local government policies. That is really all one can say about it.

Introductory Words to a
Eurythmy Performance

DORNACH, APRIL 15, 1923

Once again we would like to try to give you an impression of eurythmy. It is an artistic movement that draws on previously unfamiliar sources and makes use of a new language of forms. Therefore it may be appropriate to say a few words first. I do not intend to explain the performance, which would be inartistic. Every art must speak for itself, and, one should especially not attempt detailed explanations of an art form created to be seen. It should simply be watched.

You will see human figures performing gesture-like movements on stage, primarily with their arms and hands—the most expressive of our limbs—but also with other members of the human organism. You will see individual figures as well as groups of eurythmists, the groups spread in certain spatial relationships and performing various forms and patterns as they move around. None of all these movements and gestures, however, should be viewed as arbitrary or fortuitous, because they are intended to communicate a definite, visible language, or visible music.[1] This is why eurythmy is accompanied either by

---

1. See Rudolf Steiner, *An Introduction to Eurythmy,* Anthroposophic Press, Hudson, NY, 1984; and *Eurythmy as Visible Speech,* Rudolf Steiner Press, London, 1984.

recitation and declamation—as in the case of poetry—or by various kinds of music.

During the course of life, a human being progresses from the first babbling sounds of a baby, which express only feelings and sensations in primitive form, to articulated speech later on. Similarly, it is also possible to progress from the primitive and natural gestures ("babbling gestures," I would call them) of ordinary life, which lend clarity, emphasis, or feeling to the spoken word, toward a visible form of speech, created by movements of the entire human organism.

Therefore, what you are about to see on stage is not based on artificially contrived movements, but on exact and careful study (according to Goethe's method of what he called "sensible-supersensible seeing") of how the spoken word and human song come to be; because, in this case also, one is involved with a kind of gesturing. This form of gesturing, however, does not occur within the ordinary visible human organism, but within the outflowing breath. Naturally, the breath is always directed, partly by human will forces aided by the relevant physical organs, and partly by human thought.

We know that, in speaking, air is moved. If we made a detailed study of the forms of these air movements through which human beings communicate with each another, we would find that a definite flow-form of outstreaming air corresponds to each sound, to each word figuration and to the configuration of each sentence.

Air-forms that flow out more radially from a speaking person arise from the region of the human will, though always through the agency of physical organs, of course, as already mentioned. Sounds that shape these air-gestures into waves of a more "cross-sectional" type—if I may use such a term—stem from human thinking. If we could see these moving-air gestures, just as we can see the human being in motion (and this is possible through sensible-supersensible seeing) we would be presented with a kind of air-image of the human being, or at least of part of the human being. And within this image we would see movement, the movement of flowing air.

These air movements are being studied carefully. But instead of letting the larynx and the other speech organs transform the air-gestures into speech or song, they are turned into gestures performed by the arms, the hands, or the entire human figure, and also by groups of eurythmists moving in specific patterns. Through this arrangement, what happens in ordinary speech or song has now been made visible, and the only difference is that the thought element has been left out of these movements. The thought element always tends to be inartistic and prosaic.

Poets have to struggle against the thought element to express themselves artistically through the medium of language. They have to extract from the thought sphere what language offers them. In a certain sense they try to loosen thoughts from language, retaining only its will element, which they then use to express their soul experiences.

This is why we do not express the more undulating forms of air gestures, which emanate from the thoughts, but rather those that stream radially outward in sound, word, or sentence formation. In performing the appropriate eurythmy movements that accompany the spoken word, a unique opportunity is presented for outwardly expressing, clearly and visibly, what poets have experienced within the soul.

The belief that human souls and spirits are linked to any particular part of the physical body is certainly a kind of prejudice, because in reality the human soul permeates completely the entire organism, even the outermost periphery. It lives in everything expressed outwardly, in every physical manifestation.

Poets experience the meaning of a poem with their entire being, but, strictly speaking, they have to restrain what wants to flow into their limbs. Admittedly, there are only a few poets who really go through this experience. I think one could safely say that of everything being produced in the art of poetry, some ninety-nine percent could just as well be ignored without causing too great a loss in the field of art. But any deeply experienced poetry is encountered by the whole human being, and then soul and spirit are pouring into the individual's entire being. What a poet tries to accomplish through imagination, through the formative, pictorial qualities of sound formation, or through the element of rhythm and beat, as well as through the musical and thematic treatment of sound production, is all achieved basically by allowing the prose meaning of the words to recede, while giving voice to what is truly poetic and artistic. Consequently, for the art of speech to do justice to a poet's work, it must not place the primary emphasis on prose meaning—something that has become much too popular in our inartistic time—but it should concentrate on how the spoken word is formed.

This has been strived for in the art of speech being cultivated here, to which Mrs. Dr. Steiner has devoted herself for a considerable while. If the meaning of the spoken word is stressed in speech, the result will be essentially prose. Although this may seem interesting and intriguing, because it is believed that the personality of the speaker will then be in the limelight, it nevertheless remains inartistic. The artistic approach is in the speaker's ability to bring out various qualities, such as passionate feelings, emotions, and, in the case of thoughts, communication of the ideas themselves, through the pictorial element and plasticity of the sounds as they follow one another; and this is also done through the way diverse sound-nuances mutually affect each other. This cannot be achieved by concentrating on meaning alone. For a thought to be expressed *poetically*, the form of the thought has to be toned down. The poetic quality of language has to be looked for solely in the way speech is formed.

Apart from the image-creating quality and the plasticity of speech, the essence of recitation is found equally in its musical, beat-directed, and rhythmical aspects. In prose, verses are obviously out of place, but in poetry they are very much necessary, because they offer a kind of meeting ground that, with its rhythmical and musical qualities, is fundamentally important in speech.

In the work of a genuine poet, therefore, a hidden eurythmy is already present in the way language is treated. Thus, there is nothing artificial in eurythmy—indeed, it is entirely natural— and it manifests outwardly what the true poet has subdued, at least to a certain extent. With their entire being poets want to give to the world what they bring down into earthly incarnation. But, being restricted to the medium and use of language, they must artificially restrain certain aspects of what they want to express with a full human quality. This is all released again when transformed into visual expression through the medium of eurythmy. Hearing the speaker's recitation while, at the same time, seeing the soul-spiritual counterpart (which ordinarily flows into the spoken word) in the movements of the performing eurythmists, a direct picture of the full poetic experience is received. Eurythmy really wants to make this inherent poetic experience visible through movement "painted in space."

If you want to allow eurythmy to work on the soul properly, you must not confuse it with the neighboring arts of mime and dancing; eurythmy is neither one. However, nothing derogatory must be read into my words, because the importance of those two arts is not meant to be minimized or disputed in any way. Nevertheless, eurythmy has its own and distinctly different aspirations. And if some of its gestures appear close to mime, it can only be the result of what I would like to call a "mood of mockery" or scorn inherent in the poetry, or because of an attempt to rise above a given situation. One could compare it to someone making a wry mouth or winking an eye while speaking. Any quasi-mimic eurythmy gestures need to be regarded in this light, and if eurythmists choose to make them, they are justified in doing so. However, I am not referring to the actual art of mime, but only to the odd occasion when eurythmy may slide into a style akin to mime, which, strictly speaking, is unwarranted, because eurythmy then loses its innocence.

Likewise, what I am going to say does not refer to dancing as an art in and of itself, but only to an improper aberration of eurythmy into dancing. It is certainly possible for eurythmy movements to pass over into dancelike movements—for example, if a poem speaks of a person hitting or attacking another, or displaying otherwise passionate conduct. In such instances, eurythmy movements, which are usually entirely contained within the realm of the physical body, can turn into dancelike movements. However, if eurythmy unjustifiably degenerates into dancing, if dancing invades the realm of eurythmy for its own sake, it has a brutalizing effect. Again, I am not saying that the art of dancing is brutal, but that, if eurythmy slides into a form of dancing, it is being brutalized. A genuine appreciation of eurythmy certainly entitles one to state very clearly: Eurythmy is neither a form of mime, which is communicated through suggestive movements, nor is it a form of dance with extravagant and passionate movements, no longer contained within the dancers' sphere of consciousness.

Eurythmy occupies an intermediate position. It neither indulges in ardent or exuberant dance movements, nor does it use pantomimic gestures, which always lean toward becoming intellectual. In eurythmy, expressive and meaningful gestures are performed, which are meant, in their own way, to have an

esthetic and artistic effect. These gestures are neither intellectually thought out, nor are they excessive by nature. They are neither to be explained away, nor should they be overpowering to
the eurythmist or the onlooker. Through the immediacy of its
line and through the entire mode of movement, eurythmy
should appear both pleasing and beautiful in the eye of the
beholder.

Seeing song or music expressed in movement will also convey
a proper impression of what eurythmy is. Soon you will hear
pieces of music performed in eurythmy. This tone eurythmy is
not dancing either. If done properly, it differs essentially from
any kind of dancing. It is singing, not with voices, but with
physical movements. It is precisely this singing transformed into
visible movement that enables one to differentiate eurythmy
from its neighboring arts. Seeing it on stage will help you to
gain a true idea of what I have been talking about.

Eurythmy is only at the beginning of its development, and it
will need a long time to reach some stage of perfection. This is
why, before each performance, I have to ask the audience to be
tolerant. During its earlier stages only one side of eurythmy
was developed. But, for example, we have added stage lighting
to enhance the visual effects of the performing eurythmists.
These changing colored lights on the stage are intended to
work as a kind of "light eurythmy," to serve and accompany
the movements of the eurythmists, so that the *entire stage picture* actually becomes one eurythmic expression. However,
there is no doubt that stage presentation of eurythmy will be
improved in many ways during the coming years.

One can be confident of this future perfecting because
eurythmy uses the most perfect instrument available for any
artistic expression—that is, the human being, who is a micro-
cosm, a whole world in a small space, containing all the
secrets and inherent laws of the universe. For this reason, if all

the potentialities offered by the human organism were fully realized, the moving eurythmist would essentially present a true and artistic image of all cosmic secrets and laws. The art of mime uses only one side of the human being, as do the other arts, which also treat the human individual as an instrument, each in its own way. One could say: Eurythmy does not depend on an external instrument, nor on any one part of the human being, but transforms the human entity, and especially the most expressive members—that is, the arms and hands—into visible speech and visible song or music.

One may hope that when the possibilities inherent in eurythmy have been fully developed, a time will come when this youngest of arts will find its place, side by side with the older arts, in its own right.

Regarding Recitation and Eurythmy:

RUDOLF STEINER: It is a pity that Mrs. Dr. Steiner, who has developed the art of recitation here in Dornach, has been ill these last few days, and is therefore unable to give us examples of recitation.[2] The point is this: eurythmy requires one to revive the kind of recitation and declamation cultivated in times more open to an artistic approach to speech than our present times. Our current age is hardly sensitive to artistic refinement. For example, people today would not readily understand why Goethe, like a musical conductor, used a baton when rehearsing his iambic dramas with his actors. In our time, in recitation and declamation—which have to be

---

2. In cooperation with Rudolf Steiner, Marie Steiner-von Sivers (1867–1948) developed the Goethean stage arts—that is, Speech Formation and Eurythmy. See: Rudolf Steiner and Marie Steiner-von Sivers, *Speech and Drama,* Anthroposophic and Rudolf Steiner Press, Hudson, NY, 1959.

strictly distinguished from one another—the prose meaning is usually given primary consideration. At least, since the 1890s a strong tendency has developed to assign a more secondary place to the artistic formation of speech, while the prose meaning of a poem is considered to be most important. And yet, the essentials in speech have to be seen in the imaginative formation of the sounds, in the structure of the verses, in the musical and thematic treatment, in rhythm, beat, and in the melodious themes, all of which are fundamental aspects of poetry. Through the way speech is treated, they all have to be lifted to a higher level than possible through prose meaning alone.

The feeling for the artistic element in speech has declined completely in more recent times, as some of our present cultural phenomena will confirm. For instance, I don't believe there are many today who remember, or who have noticed, which university chair the well-known Professor Curtius originally occupied at the University of Berlin. He has been lecturing on art history and other related subjects, but these were not the subjects for which he was originally engaged. In fact, he began his university career as "Professor of Eloquence," and his real task was to lecture on rhetoric. But interest in this subject waned to the extent that it eventually appeared unnecessary that he continue lecturing about it, and so he quietly slipped into another university chair. Similar symptoms can be encountered frequently today.

If the art of speech is to be resuscitated—preferably more in form of a narrative style, or as the kind of poetry developed by the ancient Greeks—and to revive also the art of declamation, which the older Germanic poetry is based on, it is necessary to do something about speech formation. This is the point.

I don't know what caused this question to be raised, but what matters is that one achieves, through the way speech is treated, what is achieved in prose through the word meaning.

Here the emphasis is not on the prose meaning, but on the way different sounds follow each other, or the uses of rhymes, alliterations, and rhythms—in other words, the element of *form* in language—which must draw out what the present emphasis on prose meaning achieves today.

Recitation is more closely allied to measure and to the plasticity of language. Its qualities are realized through either a lengthening or shortening of syllables, something that can be especially significant in ballads. In declamation, on the other hand, particular qualities are created by altering the pitch to a higher or lower tone of voice. [*The questioner had noticed that in the word greeting, the first and second syllable had been pronounced with equal stress.*] This is not a question of art, but merely a matter of interpretation. It depends entirely on whether the speaker places the main value on the first syllable or on both syllables equally; in other words, "Tell her I send *greet*-ings," or, "Tell her I send *greet-ings.*"

Question: Doesn't this shift the weight of the rhyme?

RUDOLF STEINER: This could happen only if one neglected to adapt the other syllables accordingly. It is all a question of *mood* rather than of how speech is treated.

Question: Isn't there an inherent law expressed in a person's interpretation?

RUDOLF STEINER: No; one's interpretation must remain free. It is completely possible to render artistically the same poem in the style of either declamation or recitation. There is room for a great variety of views, just as a musical work can be interpreted in very many ways. There is not just one way of dealing with a poem. What matters is its innate essence, so that when either reciting or declaiming, one no longer has the feeling of doing this with the larynx but of speaking with the air. To develop the gift of shaping air is most important in recitation. When singing, one shapes the air. When reciting there has to be the same tendency, but in speech the melody is already within the sound. The essentials have to be brought out in the way speech is treated, and not through meaning. In this context it is helpful to consider what happened when Schiller wrote his most important poems—that is, he had a general melody in his soul to which he could then write the text he was looking for.[3] One has to aim at expressing the essentials, on the one hand, through the musical element and, on the other, through the formative and painterly qualities of language.

Question: In the art of dancing, various dancers have different styles. This, presumably, is not the case in eurythmy—or are its movements not always the same?

RUDOLF STEINER: You would hardly say that if you saw very much eurythmy! Let us say, for example, that you recited a poem, and another person recited the same poem. Even if you treated the poem in the same way, from an artistic point of view there would still be two different vocal ranges, and so on. This kind of difference already shows very strongly in eurythmy, where you could soon perceive individual characteristics of the various eurythmists; for these differences are there. And if they have not yet become more prominent, it is only because eurythmy has not been developed far enough. That will happen when eurythmy has advanced to the point where

---

3. Johann Christoph Friedrich von Schiller (1759–1805), German poet, playwright, and critic; he had been a surgeon and history professor, and became a friend of Goethe.

eurythmists really become one with their art. Then a more individual interpretation will become more noticeable.

Certainly, in eurythmy all movements are based on fundamental laws. You could find a parallel in speech. If I wish to say "man," I must not say "moon." I must not pronounce an *oo* instead of an *a*. The eurythmist therefore has to make the appropriate eurythmy gesture for *a*, but this underlying law in eurythmy still permits a multiplicity of possibilities for bringing out an individual interpretation. We are not concerned here with pedantic or stereotypical movements. You will also see a great difference between a beginner practicing eurythmy and someone who has done it for years, not only in regard to movement skills, but also in the artistry demonstrated. Likewise, an inborn artistic gift will also be clearly perceptible, even more than in other art forms.

Eurythmy is essentially built into the human organism. The human organism incorporates so that—like the other arts, such as painting—it is not absorbed rationally, but nevertheless consciously, whereas dancing goes into the emotional sphere. Other difficulties may arise there. Dancing is not really purely artistic. Eurythmy is an art already.

The course participants expressed the wish to start an association in order to open a Waldorf School in Switzerland. During various discussions the question was raised about the priority to be given the rebuilding of the Goetheanum and to starting a Swiss Waldorf School, since the realization of both projects seemed completely unrealistic.

RUDOLF STEINER: To build the Goetheanum again is more or less a matter of course, not just among Swiss circles, but among the wider circles of anthroposophists in the world. During the years when it was standing, the Goetheanum gradually came to be seen as something intended to represent the center of the entire anthroposophical movement. And there will hardly be any doubt among the majority of anthroposophists in the world that the Goetheanum will have to be built again. Hindrances toward this goal could come only from the Swiss authorities. There can be no other hindrances. Unless the authorities make it impossible for us, the Goetheanum will certainly be rebuilt.

On the other hand, while the Goetheanum was standing, the need was felt to open at least a small school.[4] For whatever springs from the impulses of anthroposophy must, by its very nature, find practical application in life. As you already know, many other practical activities are the outcome of anthroposophical work—for example, in the field of medicine. I want to mention this only for the sake of clarification.

Regarding the possibility of anthroposophical medicine, I also had to stipulate that, if the thought should ever arise of working in medicine on the basis of anthroposophical research, it would be essential for those wishing to dedicate themselves to such a task to be in constant touch with those who are ill through their personal care. This is why our hospitals were opened here in Arlesheim and in Stuttgart. This is only one example to show that, if any impulses in one or another direction are to grow out of anthroposophy, these and other institutions are certain to spring up from sheer necessity. And so, in building this small school, which is closely affiliated with the Goetheanum, and which we shall endeavor to keep going, we have done the only possible thing; we started it

---

4. The *Fortbildungsschule* was opened in 1921 for the children of co-workers in the Goetheanum. However, since private schools for young pupils were not permitted in the Swiss Canton of Solothurn, this edict being nullified only in 1976, it had to be closed down again. The school was reopened later for pupils fourteen and older.

because a number of parents, who were convinced of the rightness of Waldorf education, wanted to send us their children. These children were taken away from us again only through the interference of the local authorities. Due to Swiss legislation we were unable to do, even on a smaller scale, what had been possible in Stuttgart, where, due to less restrictive local educational laws, we could open the Waldorf School.

In this regard, world progress has shown some very strange features. Please do not think I am trying to promote conservative or reactionary tendencies by what I am going to say, but it is true that, inasmuch as education is concerned, there was greater freedom during the times when liberalism was nonexistent—not to mention democracy. Lack of freedom has crept in only during the times of liberalism and democracy. I do not even maintain that a lack of freedom and liberalism, or a lack of freedom and democracy, definitely belong together, but that during the course of history they have shown themselves to be closely connected. And the least free of all educational systems (shall I say "in the civilized world?") is in that part of Europe looked upon by so many West-European "democrats" as a kind of paradise—in Soviet Russia. There freedom is being exterminated root and branch through the most extreme form of "democracy" (as it is called), and an educational system has been set up that presents a caricature of human freedom and activity.

To return to our question: I want to strongly emphasize that rebuilding the Goetheanum is a necessity and that it could be prevented only by outer circumstances. In any case, it should be strived for. As a matter of course, this goal will be resolutely pursued by all those who are serious about anthroposophy. As soon as official matters have been finalized, we shall certainly make every effort in that direction. One can take only one step at a time, if one does not want to proceed in a theoretical way.

It is possible, of course, to make all kinds of decisions, and to think up all kinds of plans, but if one stands firmly on the ground of reality, this can be done only if and when there is a strong enough basis to warrant it.

Naturally, the ideal solution would be to complement naturally what can begin toward a general spiritual and social life through building a new Goetheanum, by also building a Waldorf School. But to move forward in this way, one would first have to overcome the obstacles put in the way by inhibiting interests in this country. For my part, I feel convinced that, if only enough people can be found—and here I am not thinking in terms of majorities—who recognize that such a school is necessary, it will eventually be opened. There is no question that ways and means will be found for it to come into being. Concerning the building of the Goetheanum, matters are not so simple. To bring that about out of the will-forces of Switzerland—if I may put it this way—is not so easy. This would have to be a matter of international effort and cooperation.

Primary schools, on the other hand, arise from the various folk cultures, and in such cases, neither our Waldorf teachers nor I, nor anyone else, has any say in the matter except our dear Swiss friends and visitors. And because of this we feel a great need to hear more about their feelings and attitudes about this point. [5]

---

5. This remark led to an exchange of views. As early as January 1923, in response to Rudolf Steiner's advice, the "Swiss Association for Freedom in Education" was founded in order to open a Waldorf school in Basel. Rudolf Steiner actively participated in the preparations for the formation of this association and became a leading member of it. He also worked toward opening the school. Together with Albert Steffen, he called on the Director of Education in Basel to clarify various practical points, and he found Privy Councilor Hauser helpful and cooperative. The Basel Waldorf school was finally opened in 1926, about a year after Rudolf Steiner's death. The second Goetheanum, built after Steiner's model, was begun in 1924 and completed in 1928.

After further contributions from various conference members, Rudolf Steiner was asked to speak some final words.

RUDOLF STEINER: It is our chairman's opinion that I should say a few words in conclusion. In response, I express my deep inner satisfaction about the best of will and the best of intentions that our honored visitors, gathered here, have shown during this conference. And I must say that every time we come together like this is a joyful event, because it causes those who participate to realize that what is being cultivated here in Dornach is very different from the current misrepresentations among so many people. If there are enough people who, through their own experience, come to realize how many falsehoods are being spread about what is really happening in Dornach, then the time will come when the intentions here—however feeble our beginnings may be—will reach the world more freely.

Of course, not everyone is in a position to perceive clearly the strange distortions of what is happening here in Dornach. There are moments when one cannot help feeling amazed at the lack of morality shown by the public, and at the general indifference toward flagrant distortions and falsifications, which really belong to the realm of immorality. One can only wonder how it is possible that such perversions of truth are taken in with particular apathy. Matters have gone so far that if this subject is touched on, one is almost met with incredulity.

Just yesterday the name of a person who commands a large audience here in Switzerland was mentioned. If now one feels it necessary to state that this person criticized my book *Towards Social Renewal* even before it was published—that is, before he could possibly have read a single word contained in it—the untruth of such criticism spread by a considerably famous person will hardly raise an eyebrow.[6] This is how great

---

6. Rudolf Steiner, *Towards Social Renewal,* Rudolf Steiner Press, 1977.

and widespread the general apathy is today concerning ethical matters. Through such apathy, these negative influences gather momentum. They increase tremendously.

About two years ago, a certain matter was spoken of repeatedly—that a theologian had written a booklet in Switzerland, in which the bizarre words were printed that, here in Dornach, a wooden sculpture was to be erected, which could already be seen in the studio, and which bore luciferic features in the upper part and animal-like features below.[7] The fact is that the main figure of this sculpture shows the features of Christ in ideal form, while the lower part of the carving is still incomplete. When he was called on it, the author of the booklet simply declared that he had copied the offending words from somebody else's writings; and this despite the fact that the author of the pamphlet was a well-known person in Switzerland! This incident has been brought to the notice of our circle here several times, and not without a decisive edge. But, due to the general indifference concerning moral matters, our words have fallen on deaf ears, instead of being passed to widest circles as an example of how strong the inclinations are—even in famous people—to distort anthroposophy and everything belonging to it by spreading untruths and gross inaccuracies.

Well, one could continue in this vein, but I am afraid that if I were to tell you even a small part of the untruths, real untruths being spread about anthroposophy, we could not go home before sunrise and, naturally, we have no desire for that. Nevertheless, the situation is such that it must again be pointed out how everything is becoming so difficult for us because of the falsehoods about Dornach and all that belongs to it,

---

7. The then-unfinished statue of *The Representative of Humankind,* as Rudolf Steiner called it, was still in the studio when the Goetheanum burned down. Today it can be seen in the "Group Room" in the second Goetheanum.

untruths being disseminated in most underhanded ways, and also because of the general indifference toward these perversions of the truth. I am not begging you to come to the defense of Dornach—certainly not. And yet, there is something of real significance in all this.

Many people hold the view that there must be complete freedom to express one's opinion. Certainly, everybody is entitled to a personal opinion, and no one can support this point of view more strongly than I do. It is a matter of course that everyone must be free to have an individual opinion and also to express it. But no one should spread lies in the world without hearing an appropriate and authoritative answer. It is the spreading of lies that causes the greatest disturbances in the world. To make people see this is one of the most difficult things we have to contend with here in Dornach. We have very many good friends, but the enthusiasm for defending the truth by rectifying false accounts of what emanates from Dornach has not yet become very strong. Our difficulties are more connected with these things than one might think.

For example, not long ago I was faced with a large number of lies, of untrue judgments, personally aimed at me. Since, in this particular case, it was very important for me to rectify judgments that people might form on the basis of these lies, I asked, "What would happen if, in order to disprove all these untruths, I were to submit within a short time documentary evidence, clearly set out and concisely written for quick and easy reading?" The answer was: "It would not alter the situation in any way." Here you have some indication of the difficulties that could be said to be at the root of our troubles. Rectifying the many falsehoods about Dornach, scattered far and wide, would certainly be a most desirable thing. The collection of funds for the creation of a Swiss School Association would not be so difficult if there were less distrust everywhere.

But I believe this lack of trust will persist as long as one is not in the position of placing the actual facts side by side with lies, and as long as one cannot count on a enough people who are not only capable of discriminating between truth and untruth, but who are also willing to stand up for the truth.

Things have come to such a state that, very recently, I had to say to a number of people: "To prove the truth about our anthroposophical cause would bring us the greatest of harm because we would be much less unpopular if the lies about us were correct. In that case people could vilify us without any qualms. But those who stand behind these lies about Dornach and anthroposophy know very well that they are scattering lies. Thus, to prove them wrong would cause them the greatest of discomfort. This is also how things are where personal matters are concerned. I am not exposing this situation to you merely to talk about it once again, but rather to look at it as the shadow cast by light. In order to give light its proper brightness, there has to be some shadow, and the brighter the light, the darker the accompanying shadow.

I put these things before you as the counterpart of the positive side. But just because they are there, you may believe me that it gives me all the more joy to have witnessed how so many among you have spoken tonight about your deeply-felt desire to do something for the cause represented here. In expressing my heartfelt satisfaction to you, I also wish to put the light next to the shadow, which—as already said—was placed before you only to let the light shine more brightly. Because so many of our honored visitors, dear to us, have spoken with voices of such deep concern about our anthroposophical cause, this light has been shining especially brightly.

FURTHER READING

Basic Works by Rudolf Steiner

Anthroposophy (A Fragment), Anthroposophic Press, Hudson, NY, 1996.

An Autobiography, Steinerbooks, Blauvelt, NY, 1977.

Christianity as Mystical Fact, Anthroposophic Press, Hudson, NY, 1986.

How to Know Higher Worlds: A Modern Path of Initiation, Anthroposophic Press, Hudson, NY, 1994.

Intuitive Thinking as a Spiritual Path: A Philosophy of Freedom, Anthroposophic Press, Hudson, NY, 1995.

An Outline of Occult Science, Anthroposophic Press, Hudson, NY, 1972.

A Road to Self-Knowledge and The Threshold of the Spiritual World, Rudolf Steiner Press, London, 1975.

Theosophy: An Introduction to the Spiritual Processes in Human Life and in the Cosmos, Anthroposophic Press, Hudson, NY, 1994.

Books by Other Authors

Anschütz, Marieke, *Children and Their Temperaments,* Floris Books, Edinburgh, UK, 1995.

Baldwin Dancy, Rahima, *You Are Your Child's First Teacher,* Celestial Arts, Berkeley, CA, 1989.

Britz-Crecelius, Heidi, *Children at Play,* Park Street Press, Rochester, Vermont, 1996.

Carlgren, Frans, *Education Towards Freedom*, Lanthorn Press, East Grinstead, UK, 1993.

Childs, Gilbert, *Steiner Education in Theory and Practice*, Floris Books, Edinburgh, UK, 1993.

——*Understanding Your Temperament: A Guide to the Four Temperaments*, Sophia Books, London, 1995.

Edmunds, L. Francis, *Renewing Education: Selected Writings on Steiner Education*, Hawthorn Press, Stroud, UK, 1992.

——*Rudolf Steiner Education: The Waldorf School*, Rudolf Steiner Press, London, 1992.

Finser, Torin M., *School as a Journey: The Eight-Year Odyssey of a Waldorf Teacher and His Class*, Anthroposophic Press, Hudson, NY, 1994.

Gardner, John, *Education in Search of the Spirit*, Anthroposophic Press, Hudson, NY, 1996.

Harwood, A.C., *The Recovery of Man in Childhood*, The Myrin Institute of New York, NY, 1958.

Heydebrand, Caroline von, *Childhood: A Study of the Growing Child*, Anthroposophic Press, Hudson, NY, 1995.

Jaffke, Freya, *Work and Play in Early Childhood*, Anthroposophic Press, Hudson, NY, 1996.

McAllen, Audrey, *Sleep: An Unobserved Element in Education*, Hawthorn Press, Stroud, UK, 1995.

Murphy, Christine, ed./trans., *Emil Molt and the Beginnings of the Waldorf School Movement: Sketches from an Autobiography*, Floris Press, Edinburgh, UK, 1991.

Richards, M.C., *Opening Our Moral Eye*, Lindisfarne Press, Hudson, NY, 1996.

Spock, Marjorie, *Teaching as a Lively Art*, Anthroposophic Press, Hudson, NY, 1985.

The Foundations
of Waldorf Education

THE FIRST FREE WALDORF SCHOOL opened its doors in Stuttgart, Germany, in September, 1919, under the auspices of Emil Molt, the Director of the Waldorf Astoria Cigarette Company and a student of Rudolf Steiner's spiritual science and particularly of Steiner's call for social renewal.

It was only the previous year—amid the social chaos following the end of World War I—that Emil Molt, responding to Steiner's prognosis that truly human change would not be possible unless a sufficient number of people received an education that developed the whole human being, decided to create a school for his workers' children. Conversations with the Minister of Education and with Rudolf Steiner, in early 1919, then led rapidly to the forming of the first school.

Since that time, more than six hundred schools have opened around the globe—from Italy, France, Portugal, Spain, Holland, Belgium, Great Britain, Norway, Finland and Sweden to Russia, Georgia, Poland, Hungary, Romania, Israel, South Africa, Australia, Brazil, Chile, Peru, Argentina, Japan, etc.—making the Waldorf School Movement the largest independent school movement in the world. The United States, Canada, and Mexico alone now have more than 120 schools.

Although each Waldorf school is independent, and although there is a healthy oral tradition going back to the first Waldorf teachers and to Steiner himself, as well as a growing body of secondary literature, the true foundations of the Waldorf method and spirit remain the many lectures that Rudolf Steiner gave on the subject. For five years (1919–24), Rudolf Steiner, while simultaneously working on many other fronts, tirelessly dedicated himself to the dissemination of the idea of Waldorf education. He gave manifold lectures to teachers, parents, the general public, and even the children themselves. New schools were founded. The movement grew.

While many of Steiner's foundational lectures have been translated and published in the past, some have never appeared in English, and many have been virtually unobtainable for years. To remedy this situation and to establish a coherent basis for Waldorf education, Anthroposophic Press has decided to publish the complete series of Steiner lectures and writings on education in a uniform series. This series will thus constitute an authoritative foundation for work in educational renewal, for Waldorf teachers, parents, and educators generally.

RUDOLF STEINER'S LECTURES
(AND WRITINGS) ON EDUCATION

I. *Allgemeine Menschenkunde als Grundlage der Pädagogik. Pädagogischer Grundkurs,* 14 Lectures, Stuttgart, 1919 (GA293). Previously *Study of Man.* **The Foundations of Human Experience** (Anthroposophic Press, 1996).

II. *Erziehungskunst Methodisch-Didaktisches,* 14 Lectures, Stuttgart, 1919 (GA294). **Practical Advice to Teachers** (Rudolf Steiner Press, 1976).

III. *Erziehungskunst. Methodisch-Didaktisches,* 15 Discussions, Stuttgart, 1919 (GA 295). **Discussions with Teachers** (Anthroposophic Press, 1997).

IV. *Die Erziehungsfrage als soziale Frage,* 6 Lectures, Dornach, 1919 (GA296). **Education as a Social Problem** (Anthroposophic Press, 1969).

V. *Die Waldorf Schule und ihr Geist,* 6 Lectures, Stuttgart and Basel, 1919 (GA 297). **The Spirit of the Waldorf School** (Anthroposophic Press, 1995).

VI. *Rudolf Steiner in der Waldorfschule, Vorträge und Ansprachen,* Stuttgart, 1919–1924 (GA 298). **Rudolf Steiner in the Waldorf School** (Anthroposophic Press, 1996).

VII. *Geisteswissenschaftliche Sprachbetrachtungen,* 6 Lectures, Stuttgart, 1919 (GA 299). **The Genius of Language** (Anthroposophic Press, 1995).

VIII. *Konferenzen mit den Lehren der Freien Waldorfschule 1919–1924,* 3 Volumes (GA 300). **Conferences with Teachers** (Steiner Schools Fellowship, 1986, 1987, 1988, 1989).

IX. *Die Erneuerung der Pädagogisch-didaktischen Kunst durch Geisteswissenschaft,* 14 Lectures, Basel, 1920 (GA 301). **The Renewal of Education** (Kolisko Archive Publications for Steiner Schools Fellowship Publications, Michael Hall, Forest Row, East Sussex, UK, 1981).

X. *Menschenerkenntnis und Unterrichtsgestaltung,* 8 Lectures, Stuttgart, 1921 (GA 302). Previously *The Supplementary Course—Upper School* and *Waldorf Education for Adolescence.* **Education for Adolescents** (Anthroposophic Press, 1996).

XI. *Erziehung und Unterrricht aus Menschenerkenntnis,* 9 Lectures, Stuttgart, 1920, 1922, 1923 (GA302a). The first four lectures available as **Balance in Teaching** (Mercury Press, 1982); last three lectures as **Deeper Insights into Education** (Anthroposophic Press, 1988).

XII. *Die Gesunde Entwickelung des Menschenwesens,* 16 Lectures, Dornach, 1921–22 (GA303). **Soul Economy and Waldorf Education** (Anthroposophic Press, 1986).

XIII. *Erziehungs- und Unterrichtsmethoden auf anthroposophischer Grundlage,* 9 Public lectures, various cities, 1921–22 (GA304). **Waldorf Education and Anthroposophy I** (Anthroposophic Press, 1995).

XIV. *Anthroposophische Menschenkunde und Pädagogik,* 9 Public lectures, various cities, 1923–24 (GA304a). **Waldorf Education and Anthroposophy II** (Anthroposophic Press, 1996).

XV. *Die geistig-seelischen Grundkräfte der Erziehungskunst,* 12 Lectures, 1 Special Lecture, Oxford 1922 (GA 305). **The Spiritual Ground of Education** (Garber Publications, n.d.).

XVI. *Die pädagogische Praxis vom Gesichtspunkte geisteswissenschaftlicher Menschenerkenntnis,* 8 Lectures, Dornach, 1923 (GA306). **The Child's Changing Consciousness As the Basis of Pedagogical Practice** (Anthroposophic Press, 1996).

XVII. *Gegenwärtiges Geistesleben und Erziehung,* 14 Lectures, Ilkley, 1923 (GA307). **A Modern Art of Education** (Rudolf Steiner Press, 1981) and **Education and Modern Spiritual Life** (Garber Publications, 1989).

XVIII. *Die Methodik des Lehrens und die Lebensbedingungen des Erziehens,* 5 Lectures, Stuttgart, 1924 (GA308). **The Essentials of Education** (Rudolf Steiner Press, 1968).

XIX. *Anthroposophische Pädagogik und ihre Voraussetzungen,* 5 Lectures, Bern, 1924 (GA 309). **The Roots of Education** (Anthroposophic Press, 1997).

XX. *Der pädagogische Wert der Menschenerkenntnis und der Kulturwert der Pädagogik,* 10 Public lectures, Arnheim, 1924 (GA310). **Human Values in Education** (Rudolf Steiner Press, 1971).

XXI. *Die Kunst des Erziehens aus dem Erfassen der Menschenwesenheit,* 7 Lectures, Torquay, 1924 (GA311). **The Kingdom of Childhood** (Anthroposophic Press, 1995).

XXII. *Geisteswissenschaftliche Impulse zur Entwicklung der Physik. Erster naturwissenschaftliche Kurs: Licht, Farbe, Ton—Masse, Elektrizität, Magnetismus,* 10 Lectures, Stuttgart, 1919–20 (GA 320). **The Light Course** (Steiner Schools Fellowship,1977).

XXIII. *Geisteswissenschaftliche Impulse zur Entwickelung der Physik. Zweiter naturwissenschaftliche Kurs: die Wärme auf die Grenze positiver und negativer Materialität,*14 Lectures, Stuttgart, 1920 (GA 321). **The Warmth Course** (Mercury Press, 1988).

XXIV. *Das Verhältnis der verschiedenen naturwissenschaftlichen Gebiete zur Astronomie. Dritter naturwissenschaftliche Kurs: Himmelskunde in Bezeiehung zum Menschen und zur Menschenkunde,* 18 Lectures, Stuttgart, 1921 (GA 323). Available in typescript only as **"The Relation of the Diverse Branches of Natural Science to Astronomy."**

XXV. **The Education of the Child and Early Lectures on Education** (A collection) (Anthroposophic Press, 1996).

XXVI. Miscellaneous.

INDEX

DURING THE LAST TWO DECADES of the nineteenth
century the Austrian-born Rudolf Steiner (1861–1925) became
a respected and well-published scientific, literary, and philosophical scholar, particularly known for his work on Goethe's scientific
writings. After the turn of the century he began to develop his
earlier philosophical principles into an approach to methodical
research of psychological and spiritual phenomena.

His multifaceted genius has led to innovative and holistic
approaches in medicine, science, education (Waldorf schools),
special education, philosophy, religion, economics, agriculture
(Biodynamic method), architecture, drama, new arts of
eurythmy and speech, and other fields. In 1924 he founded the
General Anthroposophical Society, which today has branches
throughout the world.